Ashlee is a brilliant writer and a wise leader, important, beautiful book. Her voice is clea going to be handing this book out left and

SHAUNA NIEQUIST, *New York Times* best

Say Good is a necessary read for anyone yearning to make a difference in their communities and contribute to a more just and compassionate world. Ashlee Eiland's words inspire us to move beyond silence and emerge as agents of change.

Say Good is a powerful and timely book that explores the vital role of our voices in today's world. With deep reflection and personal vulnerability, Eiland confronts the challenging reality of cultural, political, and relational pressures that we face daily.

As a pastor, she beautifully articulates the responsibility we all share as image bearers of God to use our voices to speak truth and advocate for change. Eiland's words echo with authenticity and wisdom, inviting readers to navigate difficult conversations and engage with hot topics fearlessly.

LATASHA MORRISON, author of *New York Times* bestseller *Be the Bridge*

Like many, maybe most, I've found myself exhausted in recent years as polarization continues to fracture our neighborhoods, cities, and churches. Truth matters, but how we embody and express truth matters just as much. In *Say Good*, Ashlee Eiland offers us the gifts of courage, conviction, and possibility. This book is an inspiring and practically helpful invitation to transcend the divides—truly a necessary work for our time.

JAY Y. KIM, pastor and author

Finally, a go-to book that offers wise direction on when it's good to speak up and when it might be best to stay quiet. In a world of hot takes and quick reactions, Ashlee's thoughtful approach to discernment is one I will be recommending for years to come.

EMILY P. FREEMAN, *Wall Street Journal* bestselling author of *The Next Right Thing*

One of the most important voices of her generation, Ashlee Eiland offers a radical path of love—one that has the capacity to build up our convictions and tear down our divisions; one that reveals community through vulnerability; one that teaches us how and when to use our voices to create a more just and humane world. *Say Good* is the remedy for what ails us.

RACHEL MACY STAFFORD, *New York Times* bestselling author and certified special education teacher

Ashlee is a voice—a voice of hope, a voice of love, a voice of peace and peace-making. I have watched her navigate the kinds of conversations she describes here . . . and do so with grace and humility. But here's the best part: She wants you to know that *you have a voice too.* For all who want to use their voice for good in this world, Ashlee provides a clear and thoughtful framework that will be useful and fruitful across an array of contexts and situations for years to come.

    GLENN PACKIAM, lead pastor of Rockharbor Church, author of *The Resilient Pastor*, and coauthor (with Holly Packiam) of *The Intentional Year*

In this important book, Ashlee invites us to walk in compassion and love while asking ourselves—*What truth do we want to return to?*

    KATE BAER, *New York Times* bestselling author

A profoundly healing, helpful, and practical road map to knowing what to say, share, and stand for in times of tension. This is a message for this moment. Never had I read a book this clear and biblical, with so many tangible tools helping readers find their unique voices and live with hopeful conviction and genuine compassion. In the eye-opening pages of *Say Good*, Ashlee Eiland writes with vulnerability, humility, and tender authority, graciously guiding us in building a more beautiful world.

    HOSANNA WONG, international speaker, spoken word artist, and bestselling author of *How (Not) to Save the World*

When injustice and tragedy happen in our world, many well-intentioned people stay silent. They want to say something; they just don't know how to navigate all the competing internal dynamics to find the right words. What you hold in your hands is an absolute gift. Ashlee Eiland's words will guide you biblically across the tightrope of cultural issues so you can faithfully discern how to *Say Good*.

    STEVE CARTER, pastor and author of *The Thing Beneath the Thing*

At a time when each day brings more division, *Say Good* is our generous guide for togetherness. Christ-centered, discerning, and vulnerable to the core, Eiland masterfully shows us how to steward our lives toward the flourishing of all. Though we swim in complexity, the answer is not to clam up *or* perpetually scream into a bullhorn. There is a better way, built of discernment and proximity. Now we have the tools.

    SHANNAN MARTIN, author of *Start with Hello* and *The Ministry of Ordinary Places*

Ashlee Eiland is the rare leader who embodies both profound compassion and expansive strength. In *Say Good*, Ashlee creates a framework to help us honor the complexities of our God-given humanity—in all our fragility, resilience, and belovedness. This book caused me to feel loved and known and simultaneously challenged and invited deeper into growth. I'm grateful for this timely message.

> **AUNDI KOLBER, MA, LPC**, therapist and author of *Try Softer* and *Strong like Water*

Ashlee gives voice to something I've been feeling but unable to articulate, especially not as beautifully as she has. In a cultural moment where it seems almost in vogue to cling to cynicism, Ashlee does a remarkable job of stirring the imagination and painting a vision of the future that is so compelling, so Kingdom rich, it's hard not to want to be a part of it.

Something else that I especially appreciate about Ashlee is that she is a practitioner. While her words are deeply researched, they aren't merely ivory-tower pontifications but the overflow of a boots-on-the-ground pastor who is doing the work.

Read this at your own risk. I suspect that this book will make you, like me, uncomfortable in the best ways and challenge you to step into a more resurrected life than you thought possible.

> **IAN SIMKINS**, pastor at The Bridge Church

Ashlee has given us a needed, nuanced guide for our fractured times. She compassionately leads us toward choosing justice, mercy, and humility in a world that often pits us against each other—or tells us our voice doesn't matter. How do we enter hard conversations with courage and compassion? Ashlee lays out a way forward, inviting us to honor God, ourselves, and our neighbors as we stay awake to the pain of the world.

> **KAYLA CRAIG**, author of *Every Season Sacred* and *To Light Their Way*; creator of Liturgies for Parents

This book is a helpful guide to remembering, receiving, and retelling the good story of God amid a very hard world. It's a hopeful invitation to participate in a more just and beautiful vision of that Kingdom together.

> **KATHERINE WOLF**, author of *Hope Heals, Suffer Strong*, and *Treasures in the Dark*

In *Say Good*, Ashlee Eiland reminds us that the words we speak have the power to shape the world we inhabit. As image bearers of God, we have power to *say good* into the chaos and help shape a world where we all can flourish. Eiland's book gives us the invitation and provides us with the practical tools to use the words we have for the good of all.

DREW JACKSON, poet and author of *God Speaks through Wombs* and *Touch the Earth*

In her book *Say Good: Speaking across Hot Topics, Complex Relationships, and Tense Situations*, Ashlee Eiland invites us to embrace authenticity and accountability with solid biblical teachings and heartfelt storytelling. Ashlee poignantly speaks to the tension and division we're living in. If you've found yourself wrestling with the ache of not knowing what to say, this book was written for you. It is timely and shelf worthy!

CASSANDRA SPEER, bestselling author, Bible teacher, and vice president of Her True Worth

Ashlee is truly a repairer and restorer—using the wounds, wins, and lessons of her life to encourage us not to give up but to find our voice and place in bringing hope and change into our communities.

JENA HOLLIDAY, artist, author, and founder of Spoonful of Faith

SAY

GOOD

**SPEAKING ACROSS HOT TOPICS,
COMPLEX RELATIONSHIPS,
AND TENSE SITUATIONS**

ASHLEE EILAND

A NavPress resource published in alliance
with Tyndale House Publishers

NavPress.com

Say Good: Speaking across Hot Topics, Complex Relationships, and Tense Situations

Copyright © 2024 by Ashlee Eiland. All rights reserved.

A NavPress resource published in alliance with Tyndale House Publishers

NavPress and the NavPress logo are registered trademarks of NavPress, The Navigators, Colorado Springs, CO. *Tyndale* is a registered trademark of Tyndale House Ministries. Absence of ® in connection with marks of NavPress or other parties does not indicate an absence of registration of those marks.

The Team:
David Zimmerman, Publisher; Caitlyn Carlson, Senior Editor; John Greco, Copyeditor; Olivia Eldredge, Operations Manager; Ron C. Kaufmann, Designer

Cover and interior illustration of lips by Lindsey Bergsma. Copyright © Tyndale House Ministries. All rights reserved.

Cover photograph of paper texture by Dan Cristian Pădureț on Unsplash.com.

Cover photograph of sand texture by Sirisvisual on Unsplash.com.

Author photo copyright © 2022 by Lindsay Fik. All rights reserved.

Excerpt from "Because He Lives" copyright © 1971 Hanna Street Music (BMI) (adm. at CapitolCMGPublishing.com). All rights reserved. Used by permission.

Unless otherwise indicated, all Scripture quotations are from The ESV® Bible (The Holy Bible, English Standard Version®), copyright © 2001 by Crossway, a publishing ministry of Good News Publishers. Used by permission. All rights reserved. Scripture quotations marked MSG are taken from *The Message,* copyright © 1993, 2002, 2018 by Eugene H. Peterson. Used by permission of NavPress. All rights reserved. Represented by Tyndale House Publishers. Scripture quotations marked NASB are taken from the (NASB®) New American Standard Bible,® copyright © 1960, 1971, 1977, 1995, 2020 by The Lockman Foundation. Used by permission. All rights reserved. www.lockman.org. Scripture quotations marked NIV are taken from the Holy Bible, *New International Version,*® *NIV.*® Copyright © 1973, 1978, 1984, 2011 by Biblica, Inc.® Used by permission. All rights reserved worldwide. Scripture quotations marked NLT are taken from the *Holy Bible,* New Living Translation, copyright © 1996, 2004, 2015 by Tyndale House Foundation. Used by permission of Tyndale House Publishers, Carol Stream, Illinois 60188. All rights reserved. Scripture quotations marked NRSVUE are taken from the New Revised Standard Version Updated Edition, copyright © 2021 National Council of Churches of Christ in the United States of America. Used by permission. All rights reserved worldwide.

Published in association with The Bindery Agency, www.TheBinderyAgency.com

Some of the anecdotal illustrations in this book are true to life and are included with the permission of the persons involved. All other illustrations are composites of real situations, and any resemblance to people living or dead is purely coincidental.

For information about special discounts for bulk purchases, please contact Tyndale House Publishers at csresponse@tyndale.com, or call 1-855-277-9400.

ISBN 978-1-64158-700-6

Printed in the United States of America

30	29	28	27	26	25	24
7	6	5	4	3	2	1

THIS BOOK IS FOR THOSE WHO HAVE GONE BEFORE ME, IN LIFE OR IN WISDOM:

My grandmother Eddie,
who spoke with strength and conviction, humor and ease.

My mom, Vicki,
who talks with the same confidence and grace today that she did in rooms where she was the one and only.

My ancestors,
who chose to speak at all and anyway, in spite of the cotton fields soaked with unspeakable horrors. Your words, your lives mattered. Because of your words and by God's grace, I exist.

———

AND FINALLY, THESE WORDS ARE OFFERED IN LOVING MEMORY OF THREE MEN I MISS VERY MUCH:

Jared C. Wilkins,
my friend, a minister of the gospel who bridged canyons with his faith.

Ryan J. Holmes,
my cousin, a sweet soul and faithful protector of our earthly freedoms.

Sidney Holmes Sr.,
my father, a man of God, an upholder of integrity, truth, and righteousness. I miss you more than any good words could describe.

Contents

Foreword *xi*

Introduction: Our Great Balancing Act *1*

PART I START WITH THE BASICS 11
   1 Balance *15*
   2 Fine-Tuning *29*

PART II PASSION 45
   3 Melatonin and Midnight Prayers [on holy discontent] *49*
   4 Minutes and Hours [on experience] *59*
   5 Eyes That Sweat [on injustice] *71*

PART III ACCOUNTABILITY 81
   6 Wake-Up Call [on self-discipline] *85*
   7 Frozen in Time [on initiative] *95*
   8 Fix Your Face [on hard truth] *109*

PART IV INFLUENCE 123
   9 "Search Maps" [on place + space] *127*
   10 Verified [on authenticity] *139*
   11 Pandemic Puppy and Paul (Again) [on power dynamics] *153*

PART V RELATIONSHIP 167
   12 Not-So-Happy Hour [on confession] *171*
   13 The Pharmacy Club [on everyday dignity] *183*
   14 Someone's Going to See That [on legacy] *191*

With Wide and Wild Thanks . . . *201*

Notes *205*

Foreword

Recently, I've been at a loss for words, and I can't quite figure out why. I've encountered a myriad of issues, both personal and professional, at home and abroad, and I haven't known what to do. I've known what I think and how I feel, but I haven't known if, when, and how to get the words out.

And then I met Ashlee, and something changed. I became free. I saw Ashlee use her voice, and that gave me the courage to use mine. Ashlee is a leader in every sense of the word. She steps into spaces that need to be filled and lights up places that are full of darkness. Ashlee is courageous, and I admire that. She's also a giver, and this book is a good gift. It's a reminder that we each have influence and opportunity. The opportunity to bring hope to hurting people and light to dark places. To be present. To grow. The chance to live, lead, learn, and love. The ability to speak.

Speak. At the end of the day, this is what Ashlee is asking us to do. We all have a voice. Whether we use it is up to us. Have you ever been afraid to share your thoughts? Maybe you were afraid of potential repercussions. Maybe you feared that you didn't have what it took. That you were not enough. We've all been afraid. Even as I write these words, pieces of me feel fear. I'm afraid that I've missed my moment. That I'll mess up. That I'm not enough . . . or that I'm too much. So I don't speak. That is, I didn't speak until now. Ashlee's words, teamed with the foundational and actionable steps she outlines here, are just the tools that you and I need to use our voices. To speak.

I needed this book. Better yet, I needed Ashlee. Her voice, her care, her willingness to be used for the Kingdom of God. As I read this book, I was changed. It was as if my fears began fading away. Ashlee's voice has a way of doing that for people. Of healing damaged thought processes and replacing them with food for the soul. Her words are a gentle but urgent reminder that we are more than what we give ourselves credit for. And that every one of our life's experiences has led us to this moment, to letting go of our fears and holding on to the truth. To say good, you must be willing to feel the fear of the moment and replace it with something deeper. A faith that better days are ahead and that we are on this earth to help usher in these better days.

With grace . . . and peace.

Sam Acho
Author, speaker, ESPN analyst

OUR GREAT BALANCING ACT

Not everything that is faced can be changed;
but nothing can be changed until it is faced.

JAMES BALDWIN,
"As Much Truth As One Can Bear," *New York Times*

"We have to say something," I whisper to my husband.

Sunlight streams through the large bay window in the front of our house. I'm sitting on the carpet, tears smearing my cheeks, messy strokes of weariness and anger.

We're new here. We just moved to this state eight months ago to take on new leadership roles. We haven't been here long enough to claim that we're trusted. Add in the onset of a pandemic, and not only are we not well-known—we're distanced.

But on this Wednesday in May, the thumping in my chest is drowning out our newness. My heart pounds in the cacophony of emotions I'm processing as a human, a pastor, a Black woman, a Black mother of a Black son, a Black wife to a Black man.

Ahmaud Arbery was shot on February 23, 2020. He'd been a star on his high school football team. His family described him as "a good, generous young man with a big heart."[1] He'd been out for an afternoon jog when Gregory McMichael and his son, Travis, spotted him and decided he resembled the supposed perpetrator of recent local break-ins. The McMichaels armed themselves and followed Ahmaud through the neighborhood. Another man, William "Roddie" Bryan, joined the McMichaels and recorded the encounter.

Ahmaud was unarmed. Later, on trial, Travis McMichael said Ahmaud was nonthreatening, never brandishing a weapon or shouting during the confrontation.[2]

In that snapshot of a moment, Ahmaud was innocent. I imagine him at peace in the moments before, the temperate Georgia air filling his lungs as he jogged. Then Gregory McMichael got out of his truck, began struggling with Ahmaud, and fired his shotgun three times. Two of those shots lodged in Ahmaud's chest.

As I sit and process, nearly three months after Ahmaud was shot, the three men involved in his murder have finally been arrested and charged.[3] Because the pursuit was filmed and perhaps because most Americans were home quarantined, the inhumanity of the event would stun some, shock others (but not all), and inspire social media posts, tributes, and calls for justice. People across the country would eventually lace up their sneakers to run, walk, and bike 2.23 miles in memory of Ahmaud.[4]

But before the posts and hashtags, before the shares and likes, my husband and I are just here: heaving and crying and sitting in the silence on our living room floor. Delwin and I sit with all of it—not all the hype, but the hurt.

Eventually, the hurt gives way to a sobering presence of mind followed by a wave of panic and a side dish of dread.

We're supposed to lead tonight.

Our church's midweek experience will be prerecorded and then streamed to our faith community, inviting them into worship and prayer. And I know I can't compartmentalize my pain and show up with a dabbed face, fresh eyeliner, and forced smile.

"We have to say something tonight," I repeat.

Say Good

When the pressure mounts culturally, politically, relationally, what do we choose to say? What about when that pressure isn't just outside us but also within us, grating and griding against our most easily bruised pain points as the most egregious of injustices?

Note that the question isn't a matter of *if*. We have all been given voices to use as instruments of truth, tuned to the sound of the same Voice that spoke life into the void "in the beginning,"[5] giving us God's image to bear, God's voice and heart to carry. This Voice led people out of bondage and into a Promised Land, into the realization of healing, restored community, and liberation. This Voice conquered death on a jagged and splintered beam of brutality and said, "It is finished,"[6] declaring that what looked like defeat was actually victory waiting to be resurrected. And this Voice has echoed across history in the throats of men and women who spoke, shouted, and even whispered into darkness, destruction, and division.

So it is never a question of *if* we'll speak. As image-bearers, reflecting the One who spoke life into the void, we carry voices within our God-given nature. The real question is *when*—and what we'll choose to say. If God, at the end of six days of work, could call that which was spoken into being "very good,"[7] then the words that roll up from our gut through our tight and dry throats and off the tips of our twisted tongues must mirror not just the urgency of human instinct but what is good—even very good.

In a world where the headlines seem to make bad news sound tame and trivial, to say good words may seem like too high a bar. But the bar is set just so because the stakes are high—as is the potential for personal humiliation, sabotage, or relational damage. We are increasingly accessible and visible, and we live connected to one

3

another and the world through social media. One line from a blog or speech gets overemphasized or undercut. A post gets reshared or screenshot, saved for later as either daily devotional or destructive blackmail. Even if we say something in private, the childhood game of telephone can take over on a public and global scale, moving from fingers to Twitter or Facebook instead of through cupped hands to innocent ears.

In the midst of all these colliding pressures, I've found myself hemmed in with fears and questions—and I suspect you have too.

- *How will that sentence be interpreted?*
- *What will my family think when they read it?*
- *How will this impact my closest friendships?*
- *Will I be seen as inauthentic? A virtue signaler?*
- *What's the point? Who cares if I say anything anyway?*
- *But if I don't, others will think I don't care. I do care!*
- *Could I lose my job? My good reputation?*

These fears and questions are loud. So we type and we delete. We record and we rerecord—one, two, three, sixteen times to get it just right. Some of us will turn the comments off. Some of us will keep the comments on, cracking our knuckles to the tune of "Eye of the Tiger," ready to respond to whoever might dare oppose us. Some of us will try to engage peaceably or privately, in a direct message or even face-to-face.

But all of us feel the stress as we try to balance our gut instincts with the realities of how and where our words will land. So why attempt this balancing act at all? Because in the circus of our world's messes, we know that

if we can call on the courage and the wisdom,
if we can scrape enough good words together,
we might be surprised by hope—even healing—on the other side.

Good words have power. Good words carry with them the potential to keep meaningful relationships from devolving into distance and dysfunction. They have the capacity to build up confidence and tear down division; to create community in the crevices of vulnerability; to shape safe havens where people are no longer anonymous social media bots to be battled but exquisite image-bearers to be seen, loved, and known.

Words have started wars. What if learning to balance our words could heal hateful hearts?

Our Inner Circus

When I was a little girl, my mother read me a book entitled *Mirette on the High Wire*, about a little girl who learns to walk on a tightrope.[8] I always thought Mirette was a little extreme. There was nothing to catch her if she fell—no net, no harness, nothing. And yet, there was a bravery to her choice I still can't shake, even now.

Mirette conquered her intimidation and fear of the tightrope . . . by walking it. She didn't think too hard about it, she didn't waffle back and forth. She decided she would walk the rope, and in walking it, she grew to trust her ability and skill. I wonder, as we find ourselves between skyscrapers of opinion, difference, and injustice, if the same could be true of us—if by stewarding our voices and having the confidence to walk into tension and discomfort, we can navigate the chaos by refusing to abandon it.

This kind of confidence doesn't happen by accident though. You wouldn't take an elevator to the top floor of Chicago's Willis Tower (it'll always be the "Sears" Tower to me) and just decide to take up tightrope walking on a whim. Instead, I imagine you'd find a *really* successful coach, start with strength training and conditioning, maybe work on your balance on the rusty red beam at the local playground. Suddenly you're in an epic eighties montage. Tentative steps precede effortless and sure ones. Amateur wiggles come before a firm frame and core that can withstand even the strongest gusts of Midwestern wind.

In the hard and necessary work of using our voice in the pressures, tensions, and injustices around us, what might paralyze us most isn't necessarily the metal beam or the height of the tower. What might keep us from stepping forward, from speaking, might just be our own disbelief in our ability to cross the expanse. Some of us are paralyzed, overwhelmed by how thin the wire really is. Others might need to discern when to close their lips.

When the tightrope no longer takes our breath away, when our skills are sharp and our confidence is high, the tension no longer compels us to make bad or hasty decisions. We might check the wind and weather conditions and decide—without shame—that today is a day to stay home and do something else. We'll know when it's the right time to get back on the rope. But to get to that kind of confidence, to find our own footing as we speak (or stay silent) in the face of looming tensions, we have to start with the slow, steady work of conditioning—and that's the journey we're going to take in this book.

Part of that work is discovering that not all voices are meant to resound the same. Some of our voices brave the silence around kitchen tables, shattering the hush with compassionate dissent, while others fill spaces beyond their wildest dreams, ringing from podiums before hundreds or thousands. Some might ping amidst the rafters of an old dusty church, while others might sway in the vaulted ceilings of an established city hall. Some will find a home in the ear of a newborn child, while others might comfort a loved one in their hospital bed. Some voices will speak; others will type or pen or strum or hum. Every one of them has worth.

Do you know the uniqueness of your own voice? What it sounds like, where it lives, what it responds to, where it rests? Do you know the good that is yours alone to say?

In the pages that follow, you'll come to know your voice and grow in your confidence to use it, to brave the height and terrain and the thin length of space between people, problems, possibilities. You'll be introduced to four strong pillars from which you can fashion balancing poles to help you more confidently discern your voice and navigate in times of tension or complexity, no matter where those circumstances may meet you. You'll find that in coming to know your voice, you'll also come to know the non-anxious gift of silence. You won't be pressured by it, but comforted; you won't be stuck, but soothed. Both speaking and silence will find you exactly where you're meant to be.

Each of us has been given a voice so we can use it. None of us are meant to lean solely on the crutch of someone else's words but to speak into the voids we are uniquely called to enter. I must use my voice. You must use yours. Without each of us finding our footing, grasping and gifting the good we are called to, the intimidation of the space between us wins. We lose out on the breath-taking expanse of what's possible. Yes, you'll stumble in the process. You may even fall. But you cannot let the possibility of risk deter the good that is uniquely yours to say. One day soon, if that day has not already presented itself, you'll find yourself processing either the sharpness of pain or the warmth of righteous anger, and you, too, might speak up: "I have to say something."

When that moment comes, you'll know if it is your voice that's needed, your time to speak. You'll no longer hesitate or discount yourself. And know this: When you take that first step to close the chasm, it won't be effortless—but it will be meaningful. It may not be perfect, without wobble or pause, but perfect isn't a prerequisite in this process of trying to build something more permanent, more vibrant and hope filled than the theatrics within our world's transient Big Top of spectacle and slander. You'll open your mouth or your pen cap, your laptop or your guitar case, and you'll speak.

So how do we know when and how to use our voices—not just to do good but to *say* good? In this book, we'll lay a foundation that will help us steward our voices well. We'll then explore four solid guideposts—what we'll be calling the PAIR pillars—that will hold us steady:

- Passion
- Accountability
- Influence
- Relationship

No matter our background or stage of life, these pillars make up our structure of discernment—what burdens are ours to carry, what stories are ours to tell. They'll help us measure how far we should choose to wade into a given controversy, how quickly we should react to a personal tension.

You may come to find that the heft of a particular pillar might leave you tired and out of breath, having expended your best effort but with no discernible results. Maybe you'll wake up noticeably irritated, feathers ruffled yet again by a disturbing headline, another school shooting, a deadly earthquake on the other side of the world, or a devastating crisis in your own backyard. Knowing which pillar is helping you and which one needs a break allows your heart to catch up to your head so you can stay engaged emotionally as well as mentally. You don't need (and should not expect) to master all four at the same time. Take comfort in the grace afforded you to focus on a given pillar as a unique season or circumstance requires.

"In the beginning" was the preamble to creation, opening the space and the deep to the possibility of life.

This is *your* beginning.

Welcome to the first step in facing our great balancing act,
in walking your calling faithfully,
in committing to say good.

PART I

Start with the Basics

Walking the way of discernment will surely invite self-imposed and unforeseen tensions, and we'll need to face those head-on if we're going to stay the course. And so, before we try any high-flying feats, we have to acknowledge the basics, the fundamentals of learning to say good, the foundations of walking in wisdom.

Even in the basics of balancing our voice and our influence, practice will never make perfect. But I can promise you that practice makes . . . better—not necessarily in the obvious spaces where complete strangers can see your progress through their accidental thumb-scrolling but in the fractional difference between catastrophic insecurity and confident engagement.

Practicing the basics helps us learn both the spaces where our voices may be sorely needed and the ones where we are humbly invited to sit still, to listen, to disengage and trust that this space wasn't ours to fully occupy in the first place. If we're not committed to that balance and fine-tuning, we'll soon find ourselves committed to one of two ends of the tightrope:

1. *Thoughts.* On this end, we feel tempted not just to have but to verbalize potentially malformed opinions to a captive, sometimes unknown audience.
2. *Prayers.* This is the side of silence, of saying nothing out of fear, apathy, or cowardice. Here, even if we believe in and are assured of prayer's spiritual power, we use prayer as an excuse to shrink away from our participation in God's work, allowing other human voices to fill the spaces where we are called to speak.

Thoughts will be intermittent at best or overwhelming at worst. *Prayers* may well be sincere, but staying in this space is inaction. God can choose to move, we may think, but God can move without us; we'll stay right here.

Neither option requires us to walk.

This walk must start with finding how to balance: knowing ourselves, learning our core, understanding our pace and space. It requires an awareness of gravity, knowing what tools help us not to fight the forces around us but to work with them. We must start closer to the ground than we'd like to admit, exercising the good of our voices for the first time not before captive crowds of thousands but in arenas far less famous or flashy: the family cookout when an uncle says something sexist, the playground when your child is the bully and not the friend.

The basics help us learn steadiness. The basics help us not to react wildly to the wobbles and winds but to know we can hold fast when they come. When a headline hits our hearts like a ton of bricks or when news from the other end of the phone rings in our ears like high-pitched horror, the basics help us ground our voices in peaceable presence. We no longer anxiously react but lovingly respond—because the basics help hold us still.

CHAPTER 1

BALANCE

*Your hand opens and closes and opens and closes. If it were always
a fist or always stretched open, you would be paralysed. Your
deepest presence is in every small contracting and expanding,
the two as beautifully balanced and coordinated as birdwings.*

RUMI,
"Birdwings"

Do you read the word *balance* as a noun or a verb?

As a child, I had an intense love-hate relationship with the seesaw.
Back in the nineties, when playground structure safety wasn't a high
priority, seesaws were made of either heinie-scorching metal or—
in the case of my playground—wood. The beams would scrape the
insides of my thighs as I crouched low, feet firmly planted on wood
chips or dusty dirt as I waited for a friend to struggle up onto the
other side. Then one of us would use all our prepubescent strength
to launch ourselves into the air. We'd bound up, then brace ourselves
at the bottom, up and down and up and down.

I was never only ever pushing away, nor was I perpetually floating above the earth. For the seesaw to work, you had to do both.
Too much pushing, and you'd tire out easily. No pushing at all, and

everything would come to a sad, anticlimactic end, one person swinging a leg up and off as the other crouched, alone and leg-splintered. Balance was the point.

If you assume *balance* is a noun, it becomes an inanimate aspiration or object, such as when we speak of the ever-elusive "work-life balance" or when I watch one of my daughters mount a beam at gymnastics. We can't always feel the balance, but we know it's something to be conquered. We don't always know what balance looks like, but we hope we'll figure it out as we go: a little more self-care, a little less clutter; a little more water intake, a little less alcohol; more devotional time, less doomscrolling on social media. Balance. The noun.

But if we are going to steward our own voices well and for good, balance must be a verb.

One day at work in the summer of 2022, I stood up from my desk—and the world tilted. I found it hard to stand upright, so I grabbed the doorframe behind me, steadied myself with a firm grip on the cold beam, and then carefully proceeded forward in an attempt to reach the restroom. But each step I took only keeled me further and further into a panicked discombobulation.

I had to make a decision: Either I needed to sit back down, or I had to balance myself and search for help. I chose the latter. And so from the farthest northern stretch of our office's hallway, I began the impossibly long walk to find my husband, who was also on our staff team. With every couple of steps, I moved my hand along the cubicle walls to my left, my fingertips sometimes touching more cold gray metal, sometimes grazing the rough surface of textured fabric. With most of my weight on my left hand, I paused in between gaps, mustering the energy and focus to balance until I reached the next stretch of wall.

As I finally made it to the main office entrance, the room continued to spin. I lay down and waited for staff members to call my husband—and an ambulance. I could walk no farther. All I could do was lie there and wait.

Balance was the vivid verb and not the aspirational noun to me that day. It was a series of actions and movement and careful steps in the midst of disorientation. And the same happens when we enter into tension and conflict and complexity. Balance becomes an action, a movement, a series of choices and careful steps into the world that we attend to and negotiate and tweak.

If we're going to walk our words toward good, we're going to need to balance.

Find Your Center

If you google any "how to walk on a tightrope" video, you'll likely hear someone mention the importance of your center of mass. To balance effectively, a tightrope walker must keep his or her center of mass over the rope. Any movement to the left or right, and the rope will begin to swing back and forth.[1]

Somewhere, at some time—and maybe that time is now—each of us has lost our center. Perhaps you feel like you're spiraling into the doorframe of your life without much explanation or any sense of control. Your family is in shambles; your friendships are shallow or nonexistent; your career is stagnant; you don't feel as sharp as you used to. Maybe you're like me at the time of this writing, navigating an unexpected health crisis that has left you exhausted and eager for some kind of way forward. The invitation? **Come back to center.**

But more than that, we are part of collective humanity, and I venture to say that there, too, we have lost our center. In our Western, American culture. Our two-party political system. The multiple splits and factions within church denominations. We are nation against nation, migrants and refugees and natural-born citizens. The large *we* encircles us like gusts of wind, shaking the wire and tilting the poles in our hands.

The larger *we* must come back to center too.

But what exactly determines that center?

For some of us, it's our values, the ideals that matter most to us. "Faith, family, football!" the good Texan in me might say. But our center is more than just a pithy phrase. Finding our center means knowing the core truths we can lean on when life gets dizzying. What do you believe that will hold fast, no matter the outside forces or surprises? Those are the truths my father would say "you know that you know that you know."

Before we outwardly offer our voices to the world, before we speak into the work of justice or compassion or advocacy, we must establish our inward center.

So I ask you: What truth do you come back to?

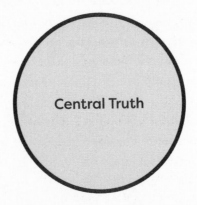

This is the center I come back to: the character of One I know whose character doesn't change, whose steadiness is forever. I still hear the low, rumbling tenor of my maternal grandmother, even though she's been gone from this earth for over seven years:

> *Because He lives*
> *I can face tomorrow*
> *Because He lives*
> *All fear is gone*
> *Because I know*
> *He holds the future*
> *And life is worth the living*
> *Just because He lives*[2]

Her belief in those words tethered my faith to a core truth not new to me, one that existed beyond and before I or that song ever did. That deeper truth stretches back through the annals of my family's history: through a dusty town in the middle of Texas, beyond a generation facing the threatening gusts of the Civil Rights Movement of the 1950s and 1960s and the Great Depression of the 1920s and 1930s, and all the way back to the transatlantic slave trade to the shores of the western horn of Africa. In those words, I hear echoes from the Holy Bible, from Lamentations, a book whose very name echoes hardship and struggle:

> The steadfast love of the LORD never ceases;
>> his mercies never come to an end;
> they are new every morning;
>> great is your faithfulness.[3]

Your center may be different—whether a meaningful religious conviction, a set of values or principles you were taught at a younger age, or some other source—but it must come with you over whatever canyon you're crossing. If you don't hold your center as you step into whatever lies ahead, shallow or quick quips become words you wish you could take back. Insults or ill-informed monologues hinder the hope for trust or restored relationship. Only that core truth can carry you as you're practicing, swaying back and forth, or even falling. Only that core truth, your security and your reason, will remain secure in the face of whatever tests it.

Strengthen Your Core

I roll over on the mat, out of breath and irritated. The instructor on the screen smiles and waves goodbye to her online audience, but I'm still heaving and huffing, waiting for my heartbeat to calm itself. That delightfully toned woman hardly broke a sweat while having the audacity to tell me what to do. After twenty minutes of crunches, bird-dogs, toe touches, and hollow rocks, the pit of my stomach feels sore and useless. I have no more in me. But still—I know that, over time, I'll thank myself for checking off another grueling core workout.

You see, according to Harvard Health,

> Your core stabilizes your body, allowing you to move in any direction, even on the bumpiest terrain, or stand in one spot without losing your balance. Viewed this way, core exercises can lessen your risk of falling.[4]

Any direction? On the bumpiest terrain? That means balancing on a tightrope isn't necessarily only about inertia, acceleration, or friction. It's not even about our feet. A whole group of muscles toward the center of our bodies—including our abdominals, obliques, pelvic floor, back, spine, glutes, and diaphragm—help usher us forward.

If we need our center to ground us, we must also have a support structure to both strengthen and reenforce that central truth. The support structure allows us to move more naturally through even the most tension-ridden subjects with grace and confidence. Our center gives us something to focus on; our core lessens our risk of falling into the abyss of tomfoolery that clouds our collective discernment and our view of humanity's innate value.

Find a Pole That Fits

I'm in elementary school, working on a science project that will demonstrate my freshly acquired knowledge about levers and pulleys: a hoist-up-and-down kitchen bucket inside a homemade well for my American Girl doll. I already have a tin can to serve as my well, an old cylindrical Folgers container from the coffee that my dad, a salesman, burned through in no time between routine meetings and domestic travel. I walk outside in the Texas heat, the white-patterned concrete below me reflecting the glow of our warm-yellow porch lights, and I find a twig that I snap to the just-right length. I set the stick between two popsicle sticks that rest on opposite walls of the can.

However, I'm still missing a critical piece. The beige string from my craft box rests to the side, but I need a crank, something I can turn in order to wind the string around the stick. I search in kitchen draws and cabinets, but no luck. Finally, my search leads me to our living room, and I rummage through the drawer next to my dad's regal grandfather clock. That's where I find it: a polished wooden crank with a glimmering golden extension. It's perfect.

I run back to the kitchen and begin attaching the string to both the bucket and the crank, ready to wind it around the stick and see my well through to completion. Perhaps I'll even put some water in it to see if I can earn bonus points for functionality.

My strategic dream of scientific superiority comes to an abrupt halt when my dad walks into the kitchen.

"Ashlee, what are you doing?"

"My science project, Dad."

"Not with the crank to my grandfather clock, you're not."

"This is a crank to your grandfather clock?"

"Not just *a* crank, but *the* crank. You insert it into the holes on the dial, and it winds the three weights to keep the clock ticking."

Well, shoot. The tool I thought I was using to further my creative thinking had inadvertently turned me into a petty thief.

One of the best funambulists (the term for tightrope walkers) of all time was Jean François Gravelet, nicknamed "Blondin." He began self-training in the art of tightrope walking at age four, using his father's fishing rod as his pole.[5] Eventually, Blondin became the first person to tightrope walk across the gorge below Niagara Falls, and he repeated that same act seventeen times. "He crossed blindfolded, he crossed on stilts and he crossed with his manager on his back. Once he carried a stove, stopped at the midpoint and cooked himself an omelette."[6]

But Blondin didn't start with a stove.

The pole keeps a tightrope walker steady and sure, certain of their footing. When it comes to finding our way and refining new skills across tricky terrain, we would do well not to start with a stove (or someone else's indispensable clock crank)—that situation you can't quite put your words around or maneuver with a certain level of confidence. It may seem like a good idea right now (points for creativity!), but in reality, that situation belongs to someone else who can carry the weight more wisely. **If you're just learning how to tightrope walk, you need to find a pole that fits.** Something that fits you is likely already in your vicinity and well within your reach. It's a skill or gift you have that may seem easy for you to hold before you on display, even if you've been tempted to compare it to someone else's. It's an area of expertise, a hard-won respectability. It's the strength of a safe relationship, the compassion of community. The right fit will emerge from the fabric of your gifts and not exploit your brokenness.

If you are longing to enter into hard topics and flammable conversations with any level of confidence, find courage in knowing you already have some tools at hand. You're going to have to discern what specifically keeps you steady and stable when the wind picks up and the wire starts swaying.

We might find balance with a family member or friend we admire, someone who will love us well and reassure us when stuff gets rough. Maybe we're steadied through a passion or career we've given healthy energy to, or a group of friendships we've worked hard to nurture and that we've allowed to nurture us in return. For me, my faith provides that centering point. My faith is not a religion or an object that I tangibly hold as much as it is a gift of a good foundation, solid ground where I choose to reorient myself. As the song goes,

> *On Christ, the solid Rock, I stand;*
> *All other ground is sinking sand.*[7]

The ground I choose to stand on at the end of the day, the reality that steadies me in disruption and uncertainty, is the faithfulness of the One in whom I put my trust.

Whatever your balancing apparatus, you have to be able to trust it to be a constant. Whatever helps you stay centered and steady won't necessarily be what steadies your neighbor, sister, or significant other—it has to fit *you*. It may be bigger than you, but it cannot overwhelm you. It cannot shake or break or become flimsy when the stakes are highest.

That apparatus, then, cannot be your iPhone or Android or Blackberry (assuming some of us still use those). It cannot be programmed for planned obsolescence or trick you into shame spirals. Your stabilizing force cannot suck you into unfocused mindlessness or be part of your unhealthy escape, whether that escape be through a screen or through the pages of a book. Whatever steadies you—faith in God, love for family, or pursuit of future goals and dreams—needs to be constant, tried and true.

Part of fine-tuning how we say good must be finding what supports us, what can help us find our feet again when we inevitably stumble or fall flat on our rear. When our ego is bruised and feelings are hurt, we've got to know what centers us and holds us upright, an aid we don't mind holding close, right in front of us, parallel to the very plane of our heart.

When you find a pole that fits, one that won't waver, you'll be bolstered even when you're exhausted from the grueling fight to say the good thing. You'll find the grace to begin again when you're worn and tired; inspired to keep going, even when the journey across breaking news seems darker and more narrow. You'll be strengthened to figure out the good you want to say or the silence you need to keep. When you're steady, you may sense fear up ahead, but it's hazy, small, and harmless. What's close and more discernable is courage.

Letting Go

Letting go is part of balance. When you step onto the wire, you start with very little: a fishing pole, maybe eventually a longer one to extend your mass and improve your balance, but nothing more. Everything else might need to be left behind.

Many of us approach hard conversations or divisive topics with trepidation, uncertain whether we should even be there in the first place. When Ahmaud Arbery was killed, more than one friend or social media follower privately told me they hesitated to speak up. Most were white women who sincerely wanted to speak out against murders like Ahmaud's that were rooted in a history of racism and racial oppression. But they didn't feel informed or practiced enough to know what to say or where or how, acknowledging both the need to center Black voices and their desire to be present in solidarity with those who were hurting. I could sense their deepest hope was to be proximate without being performative; to engage without egregious virtue-signaling; to be decisively courageous and not dismissive.

I could appreciate the tension.

Many of my white friends had, somewhere along their journey of advocating for racial justice, become hyperaware of the need to avoid shedding "white tears"—"a phrase [used] to describe what happens when certain types of White people either complain about a non-existent racial injustice or are upset by a non-White person's success at the expense of a White person."[8] But was there room for shared grief? For tears that stemmed from unadulterated empathy? Holy outrage about injustice and historic dehumanization?

Whether you're a white person coming to the tightrope with questions or insecurities—or a person of color coming to the same tightrope with trauma, fear, or even a little bit of apathy—the process of using your voice will ask you to let go of something. If you choose to carry a heap of baggage with you as you negotiate the first few steps, chances are you'll fall, weighed down by something you never needed in the first place.

Of course, there will be pieces of ourselves we cannot—and should not—let go of, like our integrity, our personalities and perspectives, our central truth, and our core pillars. But we'll have to examine other parts more purposefully. Some of us have histories of trauma that we've honored but have not yet fully excavated. For others, there are unexamined and potentially unhealthy motives that propel us forward, those motives serving more to numb us or distract us from the deeper issues. Do these parts serve us on this particular journey? Or would it be wiser to take a closer look at those parts before initiating what might feel like a death-defying feat? Is our trauma contained and processed enough for us to be a help to ourselves and others—or are we still too raw to access those gifts? Are we so driven that we're willing to leave a trail of bruised bodies in our wake, unconcerned with how our motivations might negatively impact not only other people but the ultimate purpose of our journey?

What do you need to let go of?

I used to think tightrope walkers were egocentric daredevils. But actually, surrendering a part of your life requires profound humility. You must be fearless in facing every part of yourself. You must go in, knowing you could fail catastrophically. You must understand just how much is outside your control. You must be patient and disciplined, knowing you'll need to endure bruises, scrapes, and embarrassment long before you'll achieve the success you're aiming for. You'll have to live with the reality that others are watching and that some of those watching might never understand.

As we approach the tightrope, we don't just need to lay down our baggage; we also need to let go of our pride. Pride will keep us from moving forward, encouraging us to stay where we are and not learn anything new, because we're fine right here. Letting go, on the other hand, means we'll have to keep moving, picking one foot up while the other stays put, over and over and over again. Sometimes we'll wobble, sometimes we'll fall, but eventually we'll look down and find that we've made progress—perhaps only to the middle, but then eventually to the other side. We'll have made it despite the odds.

In his words to the church at Philippi, the apostle Paul coaches us into the heart of what it means to practice humility on the journey:

> Let the same mind be in you that was in Christ Jesus,
> who, though he existed in the form of God, did not regard
> equality with God as something to be grasped, but emptied
> himself, taking the form of a slave, assuming human
> likeness. And being found in appearance as a human,
> he humbled himself and became obedient to the point
> of death—even death on a cross.[9]

So, to my white girlfriends who are worried about inward motivations and outward appearances; to my Black brothers and sisters who are tired, worn out, angry, apathetic; to those who are trying to figure out when to speak up in their workplaces, how to engage at holiday tables, PTO meetings, and happy hours—balance requires not an ever-enduring and tight-fisted grasp but an emptying. As you speak, are you willing not only to be the one who fills but sometimes the one who's emptied? Are you willing not only to put your foot down but also to pick it up and place it gently forward in the name of progress, even if that progress is slower than you want it to be?

CHAPTER 2

FINE-TUNING

*What I'm getting at, friends, is that you should simply
keep on doing what you've done from the beginning.*

PHILIPPIANS 2:12, MSG

Do you remember those elementary-school pages with light pink and baby blue lines, splayed out like a mini roadway, marking the boundaries for our number two pencils? I can see it now: a full row of *l*s, written enough times in a row to conjure up silly pictures in kindergarten minds. The first few were just letters, but by the fifth and sixth ones we were seeing soup ladles, fishhooks, upside-down shepherd's staffs.

At first, the exercises were tedious and all-consuming, homework worthy of our time and attention. Now we just write. Those *l*s appear four times in my full name, and I no longer concentrate on extending the length of the letters up to the top line of the "road." I don't painstakingly hook the ending ever so slightly to distinguish it from an uppercase *I*. I don't have to concentrate so intently on the form or style. I just let the letters go.

This, over time, is the beauty of fine-tuning.

Fine-tuning is the practice of repeatedly offering up our voices in good faith until we instinctually understand the impact of our words and how to use them. At first, saying good may feel awkward, forced, and tedious. But with enough practice, saying good becomes a habit, allowing us to speak into what we hope for in a form and style that feels like us.

The basics of fine-tuning come from the centuries-old discipline of tightrope walking itself. Each element gives us a place to start, a means to weigh the path ahead: the gravity of headlines and notifications, of showstopping one-liners at the dinner table, of stop-you-in-your-tracks texts. We fine-tune our approach because it helps us find our unique voice and get better at using it. Fine-tuning works out from our core into the lived reality of the road we're walking—or talking or writing—bolstering our confidence along the way.

Start Low

We're at the gym like we are most Tuesday nights. The girls rush in to stuff their coats and sweatshirts into a cubby after I've furiously lotioned down any ashy legs in the backseat of our car. As the mother of two Black girls, I catch myself trying to protect their legs and their social lives from the howling of winter wind and teammates' jokes, respectively.

At the beginning of the first rotation, my oldest confidently pulls herself up onto the high beam at the back. She bends and straightens, stylistically rolling her fists, one around the other, as she comes up to a straight-backed stand. She points the toes of one of her feet and sweeps it to one side of the beam, then the other. On tiptoe, she swivels 180 degrees to face the other way. A tentative hop is followed by her hands meeting the beam. She twists and kicks her legs up for the dismount, landing firmly on both feet.

I smile and wave to let her know I saw everything, and I think back to the days she wouldn't even touch the brown leather. At the beginning, she was too intimidated by the idea of falling.

Now, she falls off the high beam quite a bit, but I've never seen her stay on the mat for long. She gets back up with a quick bounce. And sometimes, when she is working on a harder skill, she'll head over to the low beam, the one where she started years ago, and she'll practice again and again until she feels ready.

Then back to the high beam she goes.

At the Republic School of Circus Arts in Russia, instructors teach students how to fall off the tightrope well: chin tucked, hands clasped behind to keep the head from any injuries. Because the shock of landing incorrectly can damage the kidneys, students learn to land on their tiptoes instead of their heels. And for girls, attempting some tricks too soon can damage vital reproductive organs.

How, then, do instructors help students take the risk but learn safely? They start them on a rope five feet above the ground. Only as the students progressively display proven skill in the basics does the rope get moved to nine, then ten feet.[1] My guess is that the best tightrope walkers in the world all started low. None of them thought they could become good enough to defy gravity itself.

Even as our confidence to steward our influence and enter hard conversations grows, even as we learn to appreciate and be grateful for the voice we've been given, we have to start and end with humility. Kindergartners start with repeating letters; aspiring gymnasts start on the low beam. Without humility, the path becomes laced with hubris and missteps, harm and failure, the pattern of every Greek tragedy.

If you decide to lend your voice to address a controversial topic for the first time, don't choose your best friend's wedding as your moment. Or your company Christmas party. Don't swing for the fences with a public blog post where you're "bold" and "brave" and "saying the thing no one else will" as you attack all your perceived opponents.

I also want to suggest that we be careful at the office about writing or filming what we want to say. (If you work from home, publishing a passion-filled manifesto from the comfort of your futon, tagging tags and naming names is also probably not wise.) Applying your voice on "company" time—whether the company of your workplace or the company of your own work-from-home schedule—may unknowingly transform you into a spokesperson for a larger entity, one whose leadership may or may not agree with your unique take. You do not need leadership to agree with you . . . but my guess is, you'd also like to stay gainfully employed. Humility teaches us to speak that for which we can personally be held accountable, and not on terrain that isn't ours to oversee.

If you start "ten feet up" without much experience or poise, chances are someone's bound to be hurt by your words—whether it's someone in the line of fire or yourself. Even if you're the type that doesn't mind a bump or bruise, the truth of the matter still stands: This practice, this walk, inherently requires humility.

In the Bible, Jesus tells a parable about the relationship between a master and a servant, about being given something to steward and the subsequent responsibilities. Jesus sums up the lesson this way:

> "From everyone who has been given much, much will be demanded; and from the one who has been entrusted with much, much more will be asked."[2]

Any platform we find ourselves occupying—whether on social media or in our family or with a group of friends—comes with a level of responsibility. And responsibility should (hopefully) be accompanied by humility, which does more than elevate an ego or demand one's own way. With this kind of humility, we serve others, look out for the good of all, and refuse to grasp power—whether earned, inherited, or given—just for ourselves.

Being promoted from five feet to ten isn't just about a mastery of skill. It requires an inherent respect for the height. The greatest start low: on the low hoop, the low beam, the low rope, the low vantage point of seeing yourself rightly.

When we start low, we use our own voices to proselytize our own minds, our negative thinking and destructive patterns. We begin to use our voices in the everyday, quiet places: around the lunches and happy hours and break rooms, where a fall means minor damage, requiring a bandage instead of major surgery. Starting low means practicing the disciplines of encouragement and gratitude more than wielding the sword of critique.

A thirteen-year-old girl at the Republic School of Circus Arts admitted to "trembling with fear for a month out on the rope."[3] Sometimes trembling isn't a sign that we'll be too paralyzed to act. Maybe it shows we're bringing a healthy dose of humility to the walk.

Start Short

I'm talking with a neighbor, and I can tell she is anxious. My son and I paused here midway through our walk past a row of familiar places— the brick church where our community meets Sunday nights, his friend's house where he'll surely want to stop and ask to play—and he is exploring my neighbor's yard. She's just introduced me to another of her friends, but her eyes keep drifting back to my son. He's made it from the base of her broad-trunked tree to a branch higher than the second floor of her house, the place where most reasonable five-year-olds would pause to announce, "Mom, look!" But my son keeps going. Up, up he climbs until he's five, six branches higher.

The neighbor looks heavenward at him, then intently at me. I take that as my cue.

"Oh, he's fine," I say, nonchalantly.

"He's so high up," she notes, confusion mixed with awe in her voice. She's not annoyed, just appropriately concerned. A five-year-old kid is high up in a tree in *her* front yard.

I say, "That's nothing for him. He's unusually good at climbing, perches himself atop roofs of playground structures and then has nowhere else to go."

And it's true. This tree is too small a challenge for him. But sensing my neighbor's hesitation, I call him down. He descends as if the branches are a flight of stairs, an obstacle tackled without a second thought.

I think back to the video of him taking his first steps in the hallway of his daycare—wide-stance legs, sprint-cruising in a tiny pair of baby New Balance sneakers.

All this is miraculous to me, a defiance of the constraints of his earliest days: a full-legged cast placed just three days after his birth, a major surgery, braces.

You'd never be able to tell now, watching this boy who bounds up trees and perches on roofs and wins the applause of kids twice his age at our local rock-climbing gym.

But he didn't start with eighteen-foot-tall trees.

He started with a two-foot stretch of carpet and won our pride right there.

It matters where we start. In 2013, Uighur tightrope walker Aisikaier Wubulikaisimu broke the record for world's fastest high-wire walk by crossing a nearly sixty-foot steel beam positioned between two hot-air balloons in just 38.35 seconds.[4] Impressive, right?

But in the Russian Republic of Dagestan, Ashkhabali Gasanov trains and manages the Dagestani Eagles, a troupe that's established right off the coast of the Caspian Sea. There, students practice on poles only twenty feet long.[5]

How far we ask ourselves to traverse not only tempers our expectations but allows us to settle comfortably into our confidence. Two feet of stumbling along—let's say, a short, meaningful heart-to-heart over coffee, with long pauses, a few false starts, but deep connection and mutual respect—may just gain the admiration and even the applause of those who care for you most. Setting into more difficulty and complexity without expertise and assurance—an unexpected bomb-drop at the beginning of Christmas dinner, for example—is unwise.

If you know little, it's better to keep the wire short. If you've managed to take a few steps and successfully tested your limits, you might be ready for a longer wire.

Starting short doesn't limit your potential; it stretches your perseverance.

Starting short doesn't cap your capacity; it cements your self-confidence.

Whether we're elevating the voices of those who often go unheard—those who've been forcibly marginalized in our context—or we're sitting down for the very first time to hear and listen to an experience we've never fathomed, the way we stretch our voices is not so much a test of skill as it is of stewardship.

Go Slow

It's my first cohort class for my master's in organizational leadership at the School of Leadership and Business at Judson University, and the dean is standing at the front of the room. He seems kind, but I can tell he's not easily moved by new-student energy. He means business.

As we settle into our places, the dean places a seemingly simple task before us.

"Pull out a pencil," he says.

I glance around nervously, then fish for a pencil out of my leather satchel that, at this point in my life, doubles as a diaper bag.

The dean hands the front row a short stack of papers and asks them to be passed back, face down.

"This will be timed," he instructs. "Work through it as quickly as you can in the time allotted."

I flip over the paper and scan the top where the directions are printed. Below the directions is a simple list of math equations in neat columns. Addition, subtraction, multiplication, division. I'm no math whiz, but this second-grade stuff I can do. As I begin filling out the answers, a tiny voice inside my head warns, *It's too easy, Ashlee.*

Hush, I tell it curtly. I'm confident and focused. No time for second guessing.

"Time's up," the dean announces. "Now, everyone prepare to grade your own papers. The first answer is zero. The second answer, four. Number three is six . . ."

My mouth falls open. I've gotten every single answer wrong.

When he reaches the end, the dean looks up at us. "One of the first lessons in leadership"—he pauses for dramatic emphasis—"is to have a firm grasp of your objectives so that you fully understand the scope of what you've been asked to accomplish. It doesn't matter if you've completed work if your work is not in alignment with your leadership objectives. May I redirect your attention to the instructions?"

He calls on one of our classmates—one of the only ones who didn't finish, but who actually got his answers right—to read the directions aloud. Where we saw a plus sign, we were to subtract. Where we saw a minus sign, we were to add. Where we saw a division sign, we were to multiply, and where we saw a multiplication sign, we were to divide.

Lesson learned. Sometimes, it pays to go slow.

Caution isn't something we're generally inclined toward in our culture. Risk, after all, has been built into the American dream and its vehicle of capitalism. And social media seems to encourage and even reward being less cautious as we stream out thoughts through posts, comments, and reels, and upload personal photos despite knowing that our sensitive information is likely already being misused.[6] Something in us wants to be deeply known—and some of us may not be as discerning as we would be face-to-face when it comes to who has access to the intimate parts our lives.

But when it comes to lending our voices to what is most important to us, communicating our vision for a world that is whole and flourishing, caution is vital. We cannot be thoughtful and wise while microwaving our most precious material for either public or private consumption. A steady diet of reactivity warps the hard-won wrestling, not just between the voice and the content, but between that voice and the soul it represents.

Walking our voices forward into the world must start with inward formation. If our motive is only to convince others, then we're missing out on a front-row seat to our own potential transformation—to our growth in maturity, wisdom, and discernment. Formation doesn't take place in reactivity. Formation doesn't show up through an outraged or impassioned tweet. Formation takes time. Time and intentionality must accompany our voices as they find their way in the world.

Yes, we might miss out on a trending hashtag. We may not be the first to speak in the wake of another shooting, earthquake, or divisive county board meeting. We may get eyebrow raises from those who expect us to speak, people who know us to be a close friend or ally. If we're disentangling ourselves from a habit of shooting from the hip, we'll probably feel anxious that we're not doing enough.

The answer is not *Don't start at all*. We must start somewhere. But if we want our voices to emerge from a deeply formed place, we're invited to start slow.

So wade gently and humbly into the territories you hardly know. Learn from others who go before you as your teachers, mentors, and guides. Is there someone you respect whose lived experience intersects the space into which you're eager to speak? Ask them out to a meal. Read reputable articles and books on a topic that span a wide spectrum of opinion so you can discern the space where your voice fits. Starting slow may defy societal norms and challenge your inner need for speed, but it'll hurt less.

Scripture tells us to "be quick to listen, slow to speak, slow to anger, for human anger does not produce God's righteousness."[7] What you allow your voice to say should never be about what you can prove but about what you allow your life to produce. Arguing to prove something (particularly when anger is involved) can be a

short-term attempt to validate knowledge, worth, or experience—
our right-ness or righteousness. But those things have already been
secured because of the righteousness of God. When we recognize that
our voices aren't the weapon of our self-defense but fruit cultivated
slowly and over time, we present far more than an acute opinion. Our
words become a testimony to the greater fullness and richness of our
lives—and ideally, a testimony to the greatness of God.

The Underrated Gift of Fine-Tuning

It's the beginning of the first full week of Lent, and a recent text from
our church community's daily Scripture reading has its hooks in me.

Lent is a forty-day stretch leading up to Easter, a season in the
Christian tradition that looks ahead to the Cross and mirrors biblical narratives like the forty years God's people spent in the wilderness and Jesus' forty-day temptation in the desert. In the spirit of
this season of self-denial and repentance, we fast and we pray, testing the tension between our belovedness and our profound need
for a Savior.

The text I can't shake is from the Old Testament book of
Deuteronomy. God's people, the Israelites, have been wandering the
wilderness, waiting to enter the land God had promised. And this
group of sojourners is up against some pretty seismic odds: other,
stronger nations. God reassures them, but he doesn't tell them that
their upcoming obstacles will be overcome in one fell swoop. Instead,
he gives this promise:

> "Have no dread of them, for the LORD your God, who is
> present with you, is a great and awesome God. The LORD
> your God will clear away these nations before you little by

little; you will not be able to make a quick end of them, otherwise the wild animals would become too numerous for you."[8]

The way forward *will* be cleared. But it won't happen at warp speed. They won't have a massive *carpe diem* moment. God isn't giving them a list of tasks to check off.

This path, God tells them, will open little by little.

I don't like "little by little." I like my progress sweeping and efficient, color-coded and predictable. I like to accomplish *this step* swiftly, make a quick end of things so that I can move on. Let's go. What's next?

But God whispers through this passage; a quick end is not normally the way he works.

Sometimes *this step* is a pause.

Sometimes the answer to forward momentum will be *no*.

Not *no* followed by an explanation or rationale. And not necessarily *never*.

Just *No, not right now*.

And so on this particular morning in the midst of Lent, I hear the invitation not only to fast from something—chocolate, meat, social media, alcohol—for sake of self-piety; God's words clunk around in my controlling and capacity-hungry soul until I finally understand what I need to give up.

Hurry, I write down on a yellow Post-it. I am giving up hurry for Lent.

Fifty minutes later, I feel like I'm watching the words ooze out of my mouth in slow motion: "Kids! Shoes on! Coats on! HUUUUU-RRRRRR-YYYYYY!"

That day is the latest I've ever gotten them to school. I offer an apologetic wave to their head of school as I drive away.

Next stop: doggy daycare to drop off our Bernedoodle, Chance. As I round a turn, I realize I can still manage to get in some desperately needed writing time at my favorite coffee shop before going to the office. Until—not thirty seconds later—red brake lights begin to domino ahead of me. We're at a complete standstill. I've never seen such a backup at this thruway. And worse, I'm boxed in, stuck in the far-right lane. I can't see the cause of the holdup. I can't move forward or back away. I'm just stuck. Chance huffs as if to say, *Well, we're here now, so settle in, Mom.*

And here I am, desperately operating the state of being I'd so emphatically given up just an hour and a half earlier.

Sometimes the answer to forward momentum will be no.

One, two, three traffic cycles later, I finally pass the accident.

But even though hurry has gotten the best of me this morning, I encounter something unexpected: *No* is not always forced on me. Sometimes *no* is empowering.

At my next stop, I have a chance to say no. I say no to hurriedly tripping out of the car and beelining it into that coffee shop. I check my carnal motivation to beat another caffeine-deprived human to the front of the line. Instead, I take a long, deep breath, open the car door, and step into the rain unrushed.

Sometimes, you fine-tune—you start low, you start short, you go slow—and the answer is still *no*.

Sometimes, despite your intentional approach, your deliberate steps, you will wobble or trip or face some stronger obstacles. Other times, it simply isn't your day: The conversation tanks, your energy isn't there, apathy is overwhelming your better judgment and motivations.

But the underrated gift of fine-tuning?

Sometimes you *get* to say no.

Those are the times you realize that a given cultural moment or hot topic just isn't yours to speak into.

I get to say no to speaking engagements that aren't rightly timed or in alignment with my values or season of parenting.

I get to say no to media requests for my take or commentary.

I even get to say no to external pressures to speak about every injustice or crisis, locally or globally.

In the wake of Breonna Taylor's murder in her in Louisville apartment on March 13, 2020, a stranger messaged through my personal website to dissent with my public comments. She felt that because I had chosen to offer public commentary following Breonna's death, I should also respond to other injustices with just as much urgency and fervor. Instead of ignoring the inquiry completely, I decided to strive for a "little by little" response—an imperfect no but a no nonetheless:

> Bringing attention to one injustice in one moment
> doesn't minimize or undermine another injustice. What I
> (sincerely!) love about your question is that you ask if **"we"**
> can pray and fight for those lives. The answer—yes! I've
> learned the hard way not to carry the pressure of all issues
> that others (or even just I) care about. This is the beauty
> in relying on the body of Christ. In one moment, I might
> be bringing light to injustice in one area while a sister or

brother in Christ is bringing light to injustice or brokenness in another. . . . We, together, can and should illuminate darkness and be ministers of reconciliation, pointing all to abundant life in Christ.[9]

Fine-tuning is yes *and* no. The beauty of slow is that you can check in with what is being formed in you. Let the space between an ask and your answer elongate. Inquire honestly of your thoughts, your emotions, your desires. Do they all fall in line with the transformation you sense taking place? If you can say yes to that invitation, your next words may lead you directly into saying good. But if you notice a check in your spirit, something a bit off or not quite right, a sense that that yes would be false or ill-fitting, then a *no* may be the more liberating and true response.

Which answer would lend itself to the best version of "good"—for yourself, for your calling, for others and the world?

Hold on. Let go.

Left foot. Right foot.

Slow and low and short and wait.

Moving into new, unknown, and untested territory can make the steadiest among us anxious. But choosing to be intentional and fine-tune our approach, knowing when and how we want to move forward and *whether* we want to move forward can produce good, formational perspectives—first within us and then outside us. And speaking from that place of confidence and assurance just might take us further than any ill-timed impulsive text message ever could.

PART II

Passion

God doesn't want us to be shy with his gifts,
but bold and loving and sensible.

2 TIMOTHY 1:7, MSG

There is no such thing as motivation in my world. . . .
I am driven, I am compelled, I am thrust forward by
a force so rooted inside me, so convincing, that it seems
futile to try to explain it. Although it has a name: passion.

PHILIPPE PETIT,
Creativity: The Perfect Crime

The PAIR Pillars

Passion
Accountability
Influence
Relationship

Now that we understand the basics of balancing and practicing within complex conversations, we're ready to explore our metrics of discernment for *what* we're called to speak into. Our four PAIR Pillars help us do that. And we must start with the pillar of passion.

Each person is unique, made in God's image, and given spiritual gifts by the Holy Spirit. We each have a vantage point and may have our sights set on different destinations. We were raised in different families and in different parts of the world. Our hobbies and interests and work experiences are diverse and layered and just scratch the surface of who we are and what motivates us.

We get to pay attention to the different facets of ourselves and acknowledge how they draw us deeper into our passions, whether our care for orphans or refugees, climate change or education. Our areas of passion matter—not just what they are but how we got there.

In a technologically driven and globalized society, we probably feel pressure to care about everything. But the particularities of what we're passionate about and why we're passionate about those things help us discern where our energies are best directed. In the body of Christ, one person may find herself passionate about setting tables and extending radical hospitality, while another is outside, looking for willing guests. Wisdom and self-awareness equip us when it comes to discovering where our voices might echo with confidence and strength.

How do we notice the steadying pillar of passion? There are undoubtedly many indicators that lead us in the direction of our passion, but we're going to explore three in particular more deeply in the following chapter:

- We pay attention to our holy discontent, the disordered places that we naturally—maybe even supernaturally—seem called to heal or correct. We're not just generally concerned about these places; we care specifically, compelled to deep heart investment as well as intentional action.

- We take stock of our experiences, the places we've chosen to spend our time or where life has taken us without warning. Whether a vocation or volunteer position, a career path or far-away country, our unique experiences matter. No one else's life map looks exactly the same as ours (even if we grew up in the same small town or spent years at the same workplace).

- We take note of the injustice happening in our orbit, the people who are hurting around us.

Together, these three elements join to form a precise and sturdy pillar upon which we can lean.

CHAPTER 3

MELATONIN
AND MIDNIGHT PRAYERS

[on holy discontent]

It started with a sign for our children's beloved teacher's classroom. The sign had been crafted with a child's sweet innocence and painstaking intentionality: seafoam-green paper, loosely scribbled flowers and hearts along the bottom edge, the imperfect placement of letters, a characteristic *s*-replaced-with-a-*z*.

The message read BLACK LIVEZ MATTER.

At some point, someone asked for the sign to be taken down. Soon, the incident made its way to Facebook.

On the surface, our response should be easy. Keep course, refuse to rock the boat, make no sudden changes. We've endured enough transition as a family in the last two years. We really don't need any more.

It's always tempting to let change fatigue make the decision.

But this chain of events, coupled with our growing gut-level tension and dissatisfaction, feels louder and more urgent than our weariness.

As Black parents to Black children, my husband and I, of course, have personal opinions, but we know better than to jump to quick conclusions. We don't know *why* the sign was taken down—or even who asked for it to be removed. We simply know that one moment, it was proudly on display in the classroom window, and the next it was not.

So on this day, we are meeting with the administration. As parents, we express our desire for that message—one we feel should be easy to celebrate, particularly given the demographics of the school—to be supported by leadership. As pastors, we sense this incident can be an invitation to deeper discipleship and collaborative learning.

The meeting attendees, we know, are sincere. We trust both their character and their intentions. At the same time, we are aware that other, potentially more powerful voices may have influenced the decision. Amid shed tears and shared hearts, we feel like the administration hears us, that they are motivated to pursue tangible next steps.

Toward the end of the meeting, one of the leaders says to me, "You know, everything you just shared you shared so articulately. Would you be willing to come share with our larger staff and administration?"

As the word *articulately* meets my ears, I'm transported back to another place, a basement-turned-piano-bar across the street from my first condo in the Chicagoland area. Delwin and I were dating at the time, and we were noticeably the only people of color in the place.

An older gentleman approached our tiny table and, unprompted, asked, "Have any white people talked to you yet?" My mouth dropped open. Delwin's mouth dropped open.

My next instinct was to shut down whatever this was as quickly as humanly possible. "No, sir," I said. "They haven't. But we're quite fine with that and are enjoying each other."

"Oh! You're so articulate," he responded.

Back in the school conference room, I shift slightly, though I smile and nod. "Let's connect about that training. I'd be open to it." I'm not lying. I *am* open to it.

But something isn't sitting quite right. When someone says you're articulate, it's because they—even subconsciously—expect you not to be. It's like when we call a toddler articulate, not expecting them to have an expanded vocabulary beyond their developmental stage. I'd spoken with clarity and conviction, and that was somehow surprising to someone.

This is how microaggressions work, I think. According to a group of professionals at Columbia University's Teachers College,

> Racial microaggressions are brief and commonplace daily verbal, behavioral, or environmental indignities, whether intentional or unintentional, that communicate hostile, derogatory, or negative racial slights and insults toward people of color.[1]

Microaggressions are hard to prove, but the impact they leave is devastating.

As we walk to our car, I pause and turn to Delwin. "I'm exhausted," I tell him.

Exhausted ends up being an understatement. Yes, the conversation went about as well as it could have. But in the days that follow, my exhaustion transforms from a mess of crushing experiences and little microaggressions to concretized grief. I realize I'm not just tired; I'm angry. I'm angry at the fact that three words—*Black lives matter*—are so controversial that simple words tied so tightly to my actual being are cause for debate. I'm angry that I even need to dissect someone else's assessment of me, that I'm being called upon to expend more time and labor to educate others after just doing that heavy lifting, sharing my heart in ways that I hope are understood and well received. In so many areas of our lives—at our church and particularly in our neighborhood—Delwin and I are some of just a handful of people of color frequently tapped to take on the weighty role of educators, sharing our experiences, both the beautiful and the brutal, for the sake of others' sometimes involuntary, potentially half-hearted, and often short-term commitment to awareness and growth.

Sometimes—most times, even—I'm willing. My spiritual gifts of teaching, faith, and leadership have uniquely placed me in situations to be able to say yes. I recall a silent retreat in Mundelein, Illinois, on November 18, 2016, and a specific couplet of verses from Scripture that helped bring clarity to both my "what" and my "why":

> "If you do away with the yoke of oppression,
>   with the pointing finger and malicious talk,
> and if you spend yourselves in behalf of the hungry
>   and satisfy the needs of the oppressed,
> then your light will rise in the darkness,
>   and your night will become like the noonday. . . .
> Your people will rebuild the ancient ruins
>   and will raise up the age-old foundations;
> you will be called Repairer of Broken Walls,
> Restorer of Streets with Dwellings."[2]

That new name—"Repairer, Restorer"—was etched into my core identity from that day forward, part of everything I put my energy to, regardless of job status or career choice or the size of my paycheck. Helping repair and restore is what I'm called to. It's what I'm called to when everyone else has more than understandably given up because of weariness or hurt. It's what I'm called to when I'm at risk of being labeled "too much" for some but "not enough" for others. I'm called to it when any payoff seems far away or out of reach. I'm called to it in majority-culture spaces and in spaces where I'm the only woman at the table.

But here's where we can get tripped up. Just because we can, have, or could doesn't mean we should. A sense of calling isn't the same as a passion.

What Is Passion?

Passion is more than just something we really love or feel drawn to (like having neighborhood friends over after bedtime for a glass of wine while lounging in my seventeen-year-old Victoria's Secret PINK sweatpants). It's more than an occasional hobby-turned-side-hustle (like when I was really into knitting arm scarves one winter) or a newfound skill you're accidentally good at (TikTok dances).

The English word *passion* is derived from the Latin root *passio*, which means "suffering."[3] In the early Latin translations of the Bible, *passion* described the agony and excruciating pain of Jesus' journey toward Calvary and his death on the cross. According to Dr. Cahleen Shrier, associate professor in the Department of Biology and Chemistry at Azusa Pacific University, the flogging Jesus experienced would've bruised and ripped his skin as leather strips and metal balls and sheep bones dug deeply into his muscles. He would've lost volumes of blood even before a crown of thorns was pressed into his head. And all this took place before the actual crucifixion, which is thought to have been "the most painful death ever invented by humankind."[4]

Henri Nouwen writes,

> Jesus fulfills his mission not by what he does, but by
> what is done to him. . . . It is good news to know that
> Jesus is handed over to passion, and through his passion
> accomplishes his divine task on earth.[5]

When we think of it this way, passion goes hand in hand with sacrifice.

So when we're determining our passion and where we feel called to use our voice for good, the question isn't if we really love or feel drawn to something—a field of study, a global mission, an area of the world, a group of people. The question is, instead, *Do we love that something enough to suffer greatly for it?*

There in the parking lot, my exhaustion and anger seemingly balloon beyond what I can carry, and suddenly I know: I cannot, in every space of my life, be called on only to repair and restore. Yes, I am comfortable and even thrive in places paint-rolled with tension. Yes, I am committed to the work of bridging breaches in my life—forever. But this day I realize that even though I could say yes to leading a training or taking part in yet another panel or discussion on racial injustice, stereotypes, or implicit bias, I need a space in which I can *experience* repair and restoration myself. Not as a pastor or professional Black woman in America—but, quite simply, as a parent. I want to enjoy being the room adult at my kids' school, seeing other people of color represented not just by the kids in the classrooms, but by the staff and administration.

Just a handful of days later we find ourselves on a school tour we didn't think anything would come of. We'd been told when we'd scheduled the tour months before—before the school year and before the sign—that there wasn't going to be space at the school for our oldest. We kept the tour on the calendar anyway, just in case.

And something happens when we arrive.

We experience restoration.

Instead of seeing us primarily as community leaders or local pastors, the head of school prays over us—as parents. We walk the grounds and breathe in the fresh air in the school's garden across the street. We pet the school dog and serendipitously meet the teachers who teach the grades our two oldest kids are in.

And then, at the very end, we're told, "Oh, by the way, a space opened up for her."

We leave breathing so easily. We leave with air and with peace. We leave feeling cared for—as grateful recipients, not spotlit professionals who will be soon called on for consultation.

After a long walk with our oldest to the park, processing the potential decision, we huddle in our room, knowing what the easy decision would be: to keep course, to refuse to rock the boat, to make no sudden changes. Easy would be to push through another year as not just pastors but as laborers, bearing the heavy weight of others' uncertain growth. Easy would be staying, but staying will involve a decent dose of suffering. Yes, it's something that seems to be in alignment with my "why"—but is it the best and right place for my "why" to settle in and take up space?

We decide to sleep on it—but I can't sleep.

I toss and turn and pace and pray. Face to the floor, I beg for the decision to be easier. Finally, after hours and no shut-eye, I just know. Even if pursuing my passion in one or even most contexts makes sense, that doesn't mean I'm called to live it out in *all* contexts. It doesn't have to mean I have to suffer alone. I realize how pursuing my passion of bridge-building has primarily cost me community and a sense of feeling seen, loved, and known. I want someone—a group of people—*with* whom I can suffer, if it comes to that. I want to be bold and loving and sensible with all the gifts I've been given, not cautious and hesitant, bracing myself for the worst. For all our passions may ask of us, they should be places of safety where we know the potential risks and assume them knowingly. They should be places where we feel we belong, places of respite and rest. That means we need to discern where our passion is needed and where it is not. We need to discern where we have stamina and vision to build bridges and bring hope despite the obstacles, versus where our passion is diminished in exhaustion and anger.

And so in our case, the next morning, when the sun comes up, Delwin and I decide to do the hard thing in the short term so we have the support and energy to pursue our family's collective passion in the long term. What we don't know at the time is that our decision doesn't just carry implications for our family. We think our decision belongs to us, impacting us and no one else. But outside observers will come to decide their relationship with us based on that very decision. Over the next few months, we lose friends. Invitations stop coming our way. We suffer.

When you lean on the pillar of passion, you test its stability by taking notice of where holy discontent is present in the first place. As you embrace this noticing, you'll find that even though you will surely suffer, you'll also feel more free. This is what makes passion a holy discontent: It's the intersection of your yes and the gospel, the Good News. Jesus, in being very nature God, gave an even greater yes in taking upon himself what we deserved for our sin and shortcomings—and that is what releases us to live freely in pursuit of what he calls us to, even in the face of the problems our passions will surely present to us. Our yes is ours to give, but the Good News was given to us, a gift of grace allowing us to take part in a story sealed in sacrifice and love. And so, at this intersection, you'll be supported by more than just a feeling or a sense of obligation—you'll be motivated by a mission bigger than you or your personal comfort, one lavished in a self-giving kind of love.

Testing the Pillar: Holy Discontent

1. What do you currently identify as your "passion" areas? Create a list and leave space after each area.

2. In the space beneath each passion, reflect on how, if at all, suffering showed up in that passion. What kept you engaged and motivated?

3. What in your personal life, family, community, or the world has kept you up at night? How might that restlessness be pointing you to pursue a passion or key decision? Does your holy discontent equip you to act with greater boldness and love in a passion area?

4. Look at your first list again. Now that you've explored your holy discontent, would you demote any of those original areas to a "hobby"?

CHAPTER 4

MINUTES AND HOURS

[on experience]

I'm going to go out on a limb and guess that a skilled high-wire instructor wouldn't put first-day funambulists on a wire over the Grand Canyon. That's because risk oftentimes rides the coattails of experience. The more you experience, the more confidence you'll have to take risks outside your comfort zone.

You probably wouldn't shoot for world record–breaking speeds or heights or lengths without having logged exponentially more falls and mediocre feats behind the scenes when no one's watching. Experience happens when you're "shooting alone in the gym," as my husband says. Experience is long hours and late nights, early mornings and restarts. Experience is the sum of persistence and consistency: showing up and showing up and showing up until one day you realize just how much you've given to that one goal, place, or hobby. This long obedience[1] is its own prong of passion, the suffering that's endured without an audience, the kind that's more pronounced because of how alone you can feel.

But little by little, despite the loneliness, despite what no one else sees, those long hours and late nights turn into months and years and decades. In the middle of the mundane grind of the work, you suddenly realize you're an expert. You're the go-to, the phone-a-friend, the mentor—all because you made a choice to show up when you weren't, well, any of those things. At one point, you may have been the freshman, the newbie, the intern, but you didn't let the hardships or unspectacular cadence of the showing up and going home stop you from showing up again the next day.

One surefire way of identifying our life's passions is to follow the trail around the bend of our experiences. Have you ever thought about the things you've *chosen* to spend a lot of time doing? Not because of a paycheck or a grade on a report card or midyear review—although the things you chose may have very well started off as obligations. Now you do these things because you *want* to, you *get* to. If you're trying to figure out your passions, those are the places that serve as a telling start.

In the words of rapper Macklemore,

> *The greats weren't great because at birth they could paint*
> *The greats were great because they'd paint a lot.*[2]

Malcolm Gladwell wrote about this absurd persistence in his book *Outliers: The Story of Success*, citing research that essentially boils down to this: "Ten thousand hours is the magic number of greatness."[3] To achieve greatness, you've got to put in the time. Time is what earns us experience. And experience will, more often than not, point us in the direction of our passions.

Notice Your Story

This is going to be a significant day at Blockbuster—I can tell from the moment I walk through the threshold of the back staff room. Boxes are piled high, some opened, some still waiting for the big reveal. Sleeves of covers are stacked and ready to go; the fresh plastic of title flaps reflect off the fluorescent ceiling lights.

Today we are starting the big transition: from VHS to DVD.

I'm wearing my employee-standard khaki pants and navy blue polo, thinking as usual that they could've paid just a little bit more for the soft cotton instead of the tough, scratchy kind. But scratchy cotton or no—Blockbuster is my first real, consistent job, the kind that comes with a paycheck, and I love it.

I plop my bag down on one of the chairs, and my manager smiles at me over the top of her thin-framed glasses without moving her head or skipping a beat.

"Good morning!" she says as she slashes another box open with her box cutter.

"Hey there!" I offer. "Big day."

She chuckles. "Yeah, we have lots to get through, that's for sure." She hands me a stack of fresh sleeves. "Can you start in Kids?"

"Sure," I say. "What do I do?"

"Just take these to the section and put a sleeve in the DVD case. Then find the accompanying DVDs and swap them out with the VHS versions.

I look down and see a collection of *My Little Pony* characters staring up at me excitedly from the top of the stack. Even the cartoons are eager for their new homes.

This job comes with a pretty impressive benefit: As an employee, I get to take home ten movies a week. And mine is a family that loves bonding over the big screen in our family room—whether with TV dinners in lap during the week or pizza and popcorn on a Friday night—so we leave virtually no movie unwatched. At the beginning of each workweek, I either call my parents from work to fill them in on the newest releases or get a list, usually from my dad, of which older titles to bring home for that week's viewing.

If the average movie is ninety minutes in length, as a family we collectively watch close to nine hundred minutes of movies a week. That's nine thousand minutes over the ten weeks of summer break.

Now, that's nowhere close to Gladwell's ten thousand hours of experience. But even just those nine thousand minutes of movie-watching—and spending hours in and around a store fully dedicated to that medium—did something to my appreciation for stories. Being immersed in stories for those weeks, I realize now, shaped something in my experience that points to a passion.

Only my lens wasn't the front of an expensive camera; it was a pen.

My blank page wasn't a movie's script; it was a journal.

By that point in my life, I'd spent hours upon hours inventing characters or stories in my brain, writing them out in the pages of my diaries or typing them out on my mom's old-school Compaq computer. My mom still has the first "book" I wrote the summer after third grade: an ABC book of plants and animals, fully illustrated by yours truly. Next I used the computer to create a chapter book that now reads like a really badly scripted telenovela. I also attempted to start a series of collected essays based on the *Chicken Soup for the Soul* books by Jack Canfield and Mark Victor Hansen.

Looking back, my teenage-girl self wasn't a moviemaker, but she was well on her way to becoming a storyteller.

The thing about what you're becoming, though, is that no one usually understands it at the time. Only you can be the one to notice and name the passions that have shaped you over the course of your life.

As an only child, I processed the world by writing. I didn't have other siblings to talk to, so, often alone with just my thoughts and a pen and paper, I wrote. Instead of holding a conversation with a real-life person, I wrote dialogue in my head. Instead of going next door to play dolls or dinosaurs with my neighbor and her brother, I wrote and told stories and wrote some more.

Blockbuster was just one of many environments that solidified my love for stories, one step of many that would help me make sense of my path. I was becoming a person who was passionate about human beings, about redemptive storytelling through writing.

Pursuing a passion through experience is different from sprinting after the title of "great." Greatness is a heavy burden to try to pursue and carry. But looking back, I did a whole lot of "shooting in the gym." I sweat and labored without knowing why. I penned poems and prayers without realizing I was putting in work.

And I'm nostalgically happy to report that my passion for humans and our stories is still going strong. Experience set the stage, sharpened my skills, and strengthened me for the journey I'm still traveling all these years later.

The Gift of Experience

Of course, even as a Blockbuster employee, I couldn't keep all the rentals I watched. Everyone, no matter how invested in the movie-watching experience, had to drop their movies back into the return slot for someone else to enjoy.

That's the distinction between the hustle for greatness and the kind of passion we need to talk the tightrope.

Our experiences are not just for ourselves. The hard work in the dark, the behind-the-scenes that no one else ever sees or even knows about, requires you and involves you—but does not stop with you.

Tricia Hersey, founder of The Nap Ministry, puts it this way:

> You were not just born to center your entire existence on work and labor. You were born to heal, to grow, to be of service to yourself and community, to practice, . . . and to connect.[4]

We storytellers know that as vulnerable and as gut-turning as our pursuit can be, the experience we collect is meant for far more than ourselves. Similarly, your experience in parenting, in entrepreneurship, in teaching, training, or caring for others—it's supposed to go out from you and into the lives of those around you.

We cannot separate community from our experience. As we go about our lives, people are inherently part of our experience, which means our passion will collect a cast of characters. Our community will include some usual suspects like beloved friends and family members, but perhaps also a stranger whose story influences our next decision; a child who's catching a glimpse of her tomorrow through us; an elderly man we befriend and visit at his assisted living home on our lunch break, who over time and conversation shows us there are still surprising, magnificent whimsies to behold in the later years of life. Perhaps as you step out and lean into the conversations and complexities you're passionate about, a group of teenagers will be caught off guard, swept up into wondering about the larger meaning of life and what their own future risks might look like.

Our experience isn't meant exclusively for us, just as our experience doesn't only involve us. Whether with coworkers or teammates, patrons or mentees, we live life together as observers and learners, moving in and around each other as we weave together a story bigger than our own.

Your experience, pursued and honed and crafted, has led or may eventually lead you to the fiery passion you carry into the world. That fire isn't a candle on your nightstand, flickering for your eyes alone. No—your passion is a roaring bonfire. And around that bonfire sit others, more than you know. They wait expectantly, their faces illuminated by the glow of dangerous flames. They're waiting for your first steps out of the lonely long hours and late nights. They're waiting to see what your experience might offer them.

Perseverance in Experience

When I would go on camping trips as a little girl, someone might use one of those artificial fire starters wrapped in yellow plastic to cheat and get a campfire going for s'mores or singing around. But as convenient as these little logs were, they would never be enough to *keep* the fire going into the late hours of the night as the stars came out and the temperatures cooled.

Those memories make me think about the apostle Paul, how he understood what was needed when a fire begins to falter:

I remind you to fan into flame the gift of God.[5]

These words aren't a harsh rebuke but a wholehearted reminder. The lull—or even the unexpected accumulation—of experience can tempt us into loneliness or discouragement. We'll all face times when we need to remember that our experience isn't for us, that there's a purpose beyond our passion or even our discouragement. But remembering takes effort. Fanning and sustaining flames requires work that a simple fire starter doesn't.

Young passions can spark and flare quickly, but experience calls us to "fan into flame," to endure until that experience has progressed well past hobby and morphed into our life's very heartbeat. We'll need those years of pursuit and commitment when we fall unexpectedly or feel like our progress has plateaued.

The Greek verb tense Paul uses here can refer to an action that is ongoing or habitual, which would make sense for this verb ("keep fanning it!"). To keep a fire going, we must stoke it over and over, add extra kindling, fan the air to kick up that which has died down.

Fanning isn't a one-time exertion of effort, a quick sprint, or a quick fix. Fanning is active and repeated—and it might eventually become quite uncomfortable.

Fanning requires you to get close to the very thing that could also kill you.

When our experience leads us to what looks and feels a lot like passion, that experience will require applied effort.

Fanning requires an intimacy, a closeness that reminds you why you're still there in the first place. This "why" must be so compelling that it carries you when you want to quit.

Fanning takes you back and tethers you to the very beginning, rewinding the story to its origins so you can watch the parts that had faded from memory.

Fanning helps you stay faithful.

Fanning helps you remember.

The very next verse Paul writes is the one we read when we first encountered the Passion Pillar:

For God has not given us a spirit of fear and timidity, but of power, love, and self-discipline.[6]

Fanning the gifts of our experiences into flame creates an ongoing spirit of power, love, and self-discipline. And what I find interesting is the spirit Paul contrasts all this with: not of apathy, not of confusion, but of *fear and timidity*.

Do something for long enough, and it'll find a way to scare you.

Do something for a series of years, and you may find yourself questioning whether you gave yourself to the right endeavor.

Do something for a series of years, and you'll discover that thing is changing—or that it's changed you.

You're not just racking up enough time to get tenure. You're not looking to retire early or make millions or a name for yourself.

When you're pursuing experience, minutes and hours turn into days and weeks and years. And those minutes and hours—the ones you're willing to endure and suffer for, the ones that have their hooks in you—are the ones that will tell you where your passions lie. Your first steps, your first words in tension and disruption, start with the boldness, power, and sensibilities etched in you through your experiences.

Testing the Pillar: Experience

1. What have you *chosen* to devote a lot of time to in your life?

2. "We live life together as observers and learners, moving in and around each other as we weave a story bigger than our own." How has your experience—the things you devote your time

to—included others? How might that experience empower and equip your surrounding community? The world?

3. Perhaps you're in a season when you feel discouraged or stalled. What might it look like for you to "fan into flame" the experiences given to you?

4. Create a list with three columns.

In the first column, write the heading *Experience*, and make a list of experiences you've logged, the ones that feel particularly unique to your life.

In the next column, write the phrase *Nurtured Passions*, and write out the passion areas you're able to identify as coming out of those experiences.

Title the third column *The Gift of My Unique Voice*. How might this exercise point you to the areas where your voice might not just be tolerated or appreciated but crucial to the flourishing of your community and the world?

Here's my example:

Experience	Nurtured Passions	The Gift of My Unique Voice
Job at Blockbuster Video	Humans and their stories	Storytelling: encouraging the world *through* story and through *telling* stories

CHAPTER 5

EYES THAT SWEAT

[on injustice]

It's the picture on my phone that I look at more than any of the others. The small boy is wearing jeans and a red shirt illustrated with the words SAN FRANCISCO and a cartoon rendition of a brown and white otter. The boy is perched on a wooden ledge next to a small playground. Beneath him, the grass is covered in light brown leaves you can tell would crunch beneath your feet. There's a blue, three-wheeled scooter under his right arm, and the helmet on his head is buckled a little too close to his mouth, like he rushed out the door without a second to waste.

He looks innocent and at peace.

The boy is my son. He was four at the time, resting in the yard of our old house between scooter sessions. I'm glad we captured this sweet moment, because—then and still—the kid doesn't stop. He ninjas across the bedroom with leaps and bounds. He hurtles down our steps like a crash of charging rhinos. He jumps and runs and climbs the highest points he can find. The moment captured in this picture was a rare sighting of quiet.

On May 6, 2020, I posted this picture on Instagram, along with the photo of a different young man. He's quite a bit older, maybe early twenties, sitting in a studio in front of a blue-and-white wispy backdrop. His skin is the color of chocolate, and there's a broad yet genuine smile on his face, teeth bright enough to be the central focus of the frame. His photo is clearly a formal occasion: He's wearing a black-and-white tux, and his low fade is clean-cut, his lineup straight and new.

Two Black boys. One truly a boy, one a young man.

One, at the time of this writing, is in first grade.

The other is Ahmaud Arbery.

One Black boy, alive and well.

Another young Black man, dead and gone.

Those pictures, those headlines and articles and posts in my social media feeds, had picked at a dormant, deep wound: a pang of premature fear from years before, when my first baby was making her home in my body.

In early December 2014, a grand jury ended the criminal case against Daniel Pantaleo, a white police officer, who had killed Eric Garner, a Black man. The officer had placed Eric in a chokehold, which eventually caused Eric's death. Eric was unarmed.

This decision came just days after a similar one in Ferguson, Missouri: another grand-jury case; another white officer, Darren Wilson; another young Black man, Michael Brown, shot and killed. Michael was unarmed.[1]

Though both these decisions came years before Ahmaud's jog

that fateful February day, I took to my personal blog to process. The inciting incident for my post? My husband was planning to go for a jog. He'd been wearing black sweatpants and a black hoodie—and I'd hesitated.

What if someone saw him, decided he didn't look so innocent, thought he fit some alleged description?

So I wrote:

> My anger and frustration with last week's grand jury
> decision was not at the police (because there are great cops
> out there, a few whom I know as friends and family), it
> was not at white people, it was not at the police officer
> or his department heads, but at the realization that no
> matter how much I try, I cannot change the fact that things
> like successful parents, private schools, . . . a suburban
> upbringing, . . . and a relationship with Christ won't change
> my skin color, and unless my skin color changes—unless my
> husband's skin color changes—cases like Eric Garner's are
> cases that tomorrow could be ours. From Staten Island to
> Barrington, my skin is seen first. And in some cases, my skin
> could be the only thing that matters.
>
> After the decision was announced, my husband, in his
> sadness and frustration, turned to me and said: I'm so glad
> we're not having a son." Though taken aback, I understood.[2]

I was pregnant with our daughter. And I, too, was relieved that we wouldn't be catapulted into parenting and protecting a young Black boy in an environment where, increasingly, it seemed protection wasn't possible. How would I shield him from others' assumptions and fears? How would I preserve his innocence and yet teach him, appropriately, how Black boys and men have consistently, historically, unfairly been treated as threatening menaces in our society?

The next year—the year we found out we were pregnant with our son—I found a disturbing resonance in Ta-Nehisi Coates's book *Between the World and Me*:

> Black people love their children with a kind of obsession.
> You are all we have, and you come to us endangered.[3]

My tears came not just because of anger over ongoing racial injustices and reports of police brutality. I didn't ever know if I was raging at a system or a history or the whole of a badged profession. My tears were more than weariness as I faced leading an entire, mostly white community, holding holy love for them alongside the ever-present tension: that there was so much they could never know, that they could never quite understand the beauty and the burden of my Blackness. My tears came on the other side of Eric's, Michael's, and Ahmaud's murders, because deep down the fear and the scabbed-over wound point to a truer thing:

longing

My tears come so easily because I yearn for the world to love my son like I do as his mother. He's so easy to love—*I promise, world. I promise.* I promise he's made of such good things, even though he'll make mistakes. I promise the first thing that was true about him is that he's an image-bearer. He was made in the image and likeness of a good Creator-God.

I want the world to start at that very first thing, first. I can feel the ways my body pleads for that goodness to be cherished.

My weeping meets the depths of my stripped-down, naked wanting.

My eyes sweat the sincerity of my soul's most human cry.

When Jesus Weeps

"Jesus wept."[4]

My mother used to say this prayer almost every night at our dinner table. It was just the three of us: my father, myself, and her. But all of us would offer grace before the meal. I'd offer the standard yet classic "God is great, God is good," my dad would offer more of an off-the-cuff, in-the-Spirit prayer—and my mom would round the grace out with these two simple words.

Sometimes I thought those two words were kind of a Christian cop-out, a way to more expeditiously get to my daddy's smothered pork chops and lima beans or my mom's fried fish and taco salad (yes, a side). But now I understand: These two words are less fancy fluff and more like faith boulders. They pin my experience of Jesus as fully human and fully God securely beneath the testimony of very human emotions.

Jesus, Savior of the world, wept.

Just before this shortest verse in the Bible, Jesus saw his friend Mary weeping. Her brother, Lazarus, was dead. And when Jesus saw Mary weeping, he was "deeply moved in his spirit."[5] Not like you or I would be moved by an old episode of *This Is Us*, or on the other end of a puppy commercial featuring Sarah McLachlan's "In the Arms of the Angels," or at the closing scene of Disney's *Coco*. When the text says Jesus was "deeply moved," it's likely referring to indignation. (*Strong's Greek Dictionary* defines the Greek term *embrimaomai* as "to snort with anger" or "to have indignation on."[6]) This "deeply moved" was more like an inward groaning, a stirring of spirit, a response to his friend's grief.

Mary's tears moved Jesus to tears. Could it be that whatever moves us to tears, whether injustice or grief or loss or disruption, is enough to move Jesus, too?

Jesus weeps one other place in the Gospels. Shortly after he enters Jerusalem, riding on a colt with a multitude praising God, Luke's account describes Jesus weeping over the city and saying, "Would that you, even you, had known on this day the things that make for peace! But now they are hidden from your eyes."[7]

While the weeping we encounter in John 11 is reflective of the Greek *dakruō*, which typically refers to the shedding of tears,[8] the kind of weeping Jesus offers over Jerusalem is described using the Greek term *klaiō*, which usually refers to a louder expression of grief, such as sobbing or wailing aloud.[9]

Undone, unhindered, Jesus weeps over a city he knows is missing the life he offers: abundant life for every person inside and outside its walls. In just a few days, crowds of people will shout for his crucifixion. His disciple Judas will betray him for money. Another one of his disciples, Peter, will deny knowing him—not one, not two, but three times. A handful of decades later, the city will be destroyed by the Roman military.

Jesus wept, he wailed, over injustices to come—both during his journey to the cross and upon a city he longed to be saved. The hard-heartedness of a people would perpetuate cycles of brokenness. Jesus did not want it to be so.

If holy discontent is at the intersection of your *yes* and the Good News—if it takes hold of your heart—it might just be what moves you beyond discontent to the vulnerable posture of one who weeps.

Holy discontent invites us to notice. Injustice invites us to weep.

What are you willing to weep over?

Without the aching pain of our wails, a passion created by holy discontent and sustained by experience can petrify our hearts over time. Without our tears, our hearts have few options but to harden. But when we let ourselves weep, we grow more tender to the point where our whole selves—hearts, hands, bodies, and voices—might join our rage and our grief. We learn that our weeping, in fact, is not meant to be scolded into the corners of our stories. Weeping is vital to our ability to speak good from a place of wholeness.

If you were taught not to cry, that weeping meant you were weak or less of a man, that piles of crumpled tissues meant they'd never take you seriously—remember that Jesus wept. His friend's grief was enough to move him. The gap between his hope and how a people would turn against him was worthy of his groans.

Injustices are more than simply opportunities for cathartic emoting. They create a chasm and give us a place to go. They show us where to set up next. They anchor us to a place, bringing focus and intention.

Justice Movement

When tightrope artist Philippe Petit was preparing for his walk across Niagara Falls, installing the equipment took him ten days. The trick was, he explained, not to look down—"for the movement of the waves will make you lose your balance."[10]

Weeping does not beckon us to look down and get caught up in the waves of grief and injustice until we are overwhelmed. Rather, the injustices we weep over propel us to start walking.

When I look at that picture of my son sitting on the ledge in our old yard, I think of the many faces of Black boys and men who were not afforded the dignity, respect, and humanity they were due. This grieves me, and it's tempting to let the grief weigh me down like an elephant on my chest. But I know that this weeping is more than tears: It shows me how I can grieve right alongside the heart of God. In the weeping, my heart shows it's not yet been hardened. I celebrate the tenderness.

And so I let my eyes sweat with tears as I walk forward: with a passion that's been pricked by the sharp needle of what's still broken in our world. I want the psalmist's words to be true for my son and little Black boys and girls everywhere:

> The righteous flourish like the palm tree
>   and grow like a cedar in Lebanon.
> They are planted in the house of the LORD;
>   they flourish in the courts of our God.
> They still bear fruit in old age;
>   they are ever full of sap and green.[11]

And so as I weep, the injustices of racism and police brutality call me forward—

- to collaborate with local leaders in the hopes of serving the city well,
- to grieve with a local family about the loss of their son to violence,
- to curate spaces for prayer and lament,
- to advocate for change.

Even when it feels like way too little, even when progress seems so slow, I weep as I walk forward—for this passion paves the way.

Testing the Pillar: Injustice

1. What injustices in our world have caused you to weep?

2. If you cannot identify a time you've wept over recent or perpetual brokenness in your life or our world, what keeps you from weeping? What have you been taught about expressing your emotions—particularly the emotions of anger and sadness?

3. How might the Lord be inviting you to grow in Christ's likeness by identifying with our Savior who wept? How might God long to speak to or even heal the disordered perceptions or judgments you carry around weeping?

4. As you identify injustices toward which you might direct your holy discontent and experience, what might be an immediate next step you can take to address that injustice with your voice? What needs to be said that can be said from a place of wholeness, your tender heart included?

5. How might you keep your heart tender in this work? What's the greatest threat to staying emotionally present along this journey?

PART III

Accountability

The way God designed our bodies is a model for understanding our lives together as a church: every part dependent on every other part, the parts we mention and the parts we don't, the parts we see and the parts we don't. If one part hurts, every other part is involved in the hurt, and in the healing. If one part flourishes, every other part enters into the exuberance.

I CORINTHIANS 12:25-26, MSG

Speech has power and . . . words do not fade.
What starts out as a sound ends in a deed.

ABRAHAM JOSHUA HESCHEL

The PAIR Pillars

Passion
Accountability
Influence
Relationship

The comments section of our favorite social media platforms might as well be filed under *Chaos* in your favorite reference encyclopedia: unsolicited opinions in response to equally unsolicited thoughts, all without real relationship (more on that later), filter, or follow-up. But each person is one distinct part of a larger whole. This interdependence should drive us to weigh our words, unspoken and spoken alike.

If we're going to live in interdependence, we have to be willing to allow other lives to touch and test ours. Sharpening cannot happen without friction. Neither can full growth and transformation into Christlikeness take place outside the reality of proximity, where there exists the willingness for our life and words to be tested for integrity and character and generosity outside ourselves.

We tend to ignore and discard accountability in the shallow pursuit of self-serving freedom. True accountability, though, doesn't restrict; it refines. As we consider our words and how they move in the world, accountability steadies us through self-discipline, initiative, and hard truth—and is part of producing the humility and wholeness we've been searching for all along.

CHAPTER 6

WAKE-UP CALL

[on self-discipline]

Every morning at 5:25 a.m., the alarm on my iPhone starts playing a sound called "Springtide." To trick myself into not pressing the snooze button more than once, I've also programmed our coffeepot downstairs to begin brewing at 5:35. By the time the snooze alarm rings, the smell of coffee launches me into my usual routine: take my two gummy vitamins (which I suspect really do little other than sugar me up); put away any dishes from the dishwasher or drying rack; feed the dog; pour the coffee into a mug that matches the needs of the day (anything from a porcelain calligraphed "Today I Will Choose Joy" to a florally enthusiastic "Be Present" to Moira Rose and her collection of wigs). I head to the wingback chair in the living room, turn the knob of the gas to light the fire, and splay a loose-knit gray blanket over my legs. Then I set out to open my Bible, write in my journal, and spend some time in a book (though usually, by the time I get to my journal, a child is awake and I'm persuaded out of my chair to pour cereal or boil water for oatmeal).

That post-alarm routine has looked different in various seasons of my life.

In college, I woke up to a rotation of popular songs set as my ringtone before rolling out of bed to work out at the gym across from our dorm or to cram for an exam or to start my day as an RA early with a floor resident's inquiries.

Years before, my first phone—the classic Nokia with interchangeable navy blue or lime-green cover—would chirp "boo-do-doo-doo, boo-do-doo-doo, boo-do-doo-doo-*doooo*" to tell sixteen-year-old me to get up and get dressed and drive myself the forty-five minutes to school.

When I was a young professional, my alarm woke me up for the short early-morning drive from my apartment in Glendale to the corporate offices of Nestlé USA so I could prep for the day's meetings and presentations in peace. On work trips, I called the front desk to request a wakeup call because I could never (and still don't) trust hotel clock alarms. In my newlywed years, alarms got me out of bed for early morning runs or to check in with my boss at a local breakfast establishment.

Alarms have woken me every few hours for bleary-eyed feedings of my newborn, and then for some early few minutes of quiet before my toddlers woke up.

Even as the routines have changed, the need for a reliable wakeup call has been consistent. Over and over and over, tones and tunes and songs move me from slumber into the day ahead. It's remarkable to think about how many times over the course of my life I've automatically set myself a jolt of sonic accountability. Without it, I'd surely have been late or rushed more times that I'd be able to count. I would've chosen to sleep off a lack of motivation or discouragement or grief or simply stay in bed.

When I didn't feel like getting up to work out or study or read or pray, wakeup calls got my feet to the floor and into the day. Accountability—even in small, routine ways—brings me back to my goals and hopes.

It occurs to me now that my feet hitting the floor one, twelve, twelve hundred times over the years has added up to a kind of discipline—not just for a hobby or skill, but for simply showing up no matter the conditions. That discipline has called me to a deeper personal accountability, accountability that sustains and prepares me for the steps ahead, the higher commitments.

The Tools of Discipline

On June 23, 2013, Nik Wallenda became the first person to cross the Grand Canyon's Little Colorado River Gorge. At just thirty-four years old and wearing a grossly understated blue T-shirt and jeans, Wallenda made the terrifying trek without a harness.[1] The quarter-mile walk on the steel cable took twenty-three minutes.

A few weeks before that walk, an interviewer asked Wallenda how many practices he'd do at the Canyon.

"I will not do any practices out there," Wallenda responded.[2]

It was true: The Grand Canyon walk was a one-shot, all-or-nothing. But what many people didn't know was that Wallenda had, at that point, done close to one hundred practices for it in different places and different conditions.

Just sixteen days before he would become the first person to cross Little Colorado River Gorge, Wallenda filmed one of those practices.[3]

He wasn't fifteen hundred feet above roaring waters as he would be over the canyon. Far fewer people were watching. The wire, it turns out, was four hundred feet shorter than the one that would be suspended above the gorge. Just a day earlier, Wallenda had intentionally practiced in the middle of Tropical Storm Andrea, weathering wind gusts of fifty-three miles per hour so he could simulate what he'd feel on June 23.

Self-discipline is repetition and practice, the choice of how we're going to regulate our own actions and respond to the alarms that come our way. As we discern where and how to use our voices for good—in the face of injustices, on behalf of the oppressed, in the wake of an organization-shifting decision, or in the midst of family drama—alarms could come in the form of breaking news, a text that stops us in our tracks, a call that summons us out of a board meeting, or a comment from our kid that seems more like a cry for help than a passing quip. Part of our work will be discerning what those alarms are and how we'll choose to meet them. Self-discipline gets us to the ground, to the starting lines of wires we're invited to cross.

But simply responding to alarms isn't the same as deliberate practice for the walk. Say we decide to show up: to the coffee shop, on our blog, at the brunch table. Even in having the self-discipline to show up, we have to be aware of a shadow side of *simply* showing up. A measure of accountability can quickly turn into a stubborn willpower that negates or undermines both our limitations *and* the source from which our willpower comes.

In his book *Celebration of Discipline: The Path to Spiritual Growth*, author Richard J. Foster makes this distinction clear in examining Paul's letter to the church at Colossae: Discipline that relies *only* on my presence and decision to show up will quickly convince me over time that I'm also the primary reason why I'm succeeding at a given endeavor.[4] Self-reliance leads to a lack of self-awareness. If Wallenda showed up to his hundredth practice and decided that—because he'd showed up to the previous ninety-nine—he didn't need a pole or his soft-soled shoes this time, I suspect his hundredth practice would have been a lot riskier. Without the tools and resources he'd needed and submitted to all those times before, all he would have was the idea that his decision to walk would be sufficient.

Self-discipline gets us to show up, but only tools or circumstances that we could not have conjured up on our own can sustain us through what's next. We cannot rely on our self-discipline alone.

Those of us who choose to follow the way of Jesus Christ know that the tools and circumstances sustaining our discipline are gifts of grace from God. As Foster reminds us,

> The classical Disciplines of the spiritual life call us to move beyond surface living into the depths. . . .[5]

> The Disciplines are God's way of getting us into the ground; they put us where he can work within us and transform us. By themselves the Spiritual Disciplines can do nothing; they can only get us to the place where something can be done. They are God's means of grace.[6]

We can't self-discipline our way into or out of a gift. Grace is something we receive, not something we will into being. Self-discipline is ours to do; grace is entirely disconnected from our effort. Self-discipline is part of what "gets us into the ground"; grace goes to work on us and helps right-size our impact. With this kind of gift, our only responsibility is to choose the posture and spirit in which we receive it.

We must hold in tension what we bring in the way of self-discipline with all the things we couldn't have manufactured or manipulated ourselves. Self-discipline isn't what saves us, but it positions us for transformation. By ourselves, we can do nothing. Self-discipline gets us to a place where something can be done.

Showing Up

Amid the proverbial alarms of flammable topics and headlines—will we show up?

If we're going to discern when and how to use our voices, we must discipline ourselves in practices that meet every moment. Discipline calls us to be willing to keep showing up in hard situations—when we don't have all the answers or the perfect thing to say, when the conversation isn't broadcast for public consumption, when there's a high likelihood that we'll get a lot wrong.

When we show up, we'll also have to decide what tools and resources will help remind us we cannot rely on ourselves alone. That's where accountability comes in.

Early on in our marriage, my husband and I made a commitment to do our very best not to have complex arguments or discussions with raised voices in front of our kids. And let me clarify: That's not a small commitment. You might describe the two of us as "spicy." We both have big personalities, big expressions, and big feelings. I love who we are, together and separately, but this also means our hearts can get lost in our bigness, our discussions quickly deteriorating into deep dives about someone's tone or "how you said what you said." Both of us had to grow up early because of hard things that happened in our lives. Both of us had to fight, whether for protection or to be heard. Both of us feel deeply, whether with our full bodies or expressive emotions.

Now, here's the problem: Delwin and I happen to be imperfect human beings. So even though we've named our desire not to have complex arguments or discussions with raised voices in front of our kids . . . have we still done it? Yes, we have.

But here's where we can celebrate discipline. Our commitment, even though we hold to it imperfectly, is still a resource. Even in the moments where the discussion wheels seem to be coming off, almost always one of us will grab on to that resource and restate the initial commitment:

- "You know what? Let's pick this discussion up later, after the kids go to bed."

- "Kids, Mommy and Daddy aren't mad at each other. We love each other very much and are committed to working through this hard conversation. You've done nothing wrong."

- "Hey, we said we wouldn't raise our voices in front of the kids. I care about this conversation and want to have it, but only if we can have it with a different tone and when they're not around."

This commitment, even though we don't follow it 100 percent of the time, still holds us accountable. When we identify a tone in a conversation or notice key words coming out of our mouths, we hear an alarm that calls us to show up in a certain way. No matter how our routine changes or what subjects our conversations focus on, those small interactions refine accountability. We continue to move toward being transformed for the better, both individually and together.

Another way this kind of accountability can show up is online. I've made it a personal practice of self-discipline not to argue with people on social media. Back-and-forth banter, particularly with people I don't know or will likely never meet, is hardly ever fruitful or in service of the core that drives me, the passion I'm moving toward. If I'm triggered by a post, I'll usually mute it. If someone I "know" (meaning I don't really know them personally but am loosely connected) posts something with which I disagree, I'll weigh whether to reach out to them directly, not publicly. If I'm not willing to do so, that means I've decided not to post a comment publicly. For people I actually *do* know, I can reach out to them personally via a social media message, a text, or a phone call—and again, if I'm not willing to do so, I'm not invested enough to post a comment publicly.[7]

Every time I hear an alarm—whether the tone of a conversation or an inflammatory post online—I get to decide how I want to show up and the standards by which I'd like to do so.

Because here's my hunch: For as eager as we may be to hold others accountable for the ways they choose to use their voices in the world, holding others accountable means very little if somehow everyone else *but us* needs accountability.

In the Sermon on the Mount, Jesus speaks directly to those who self-assign the right to judge others—and there's a gift in what he says. He speaks directly to those he terms *hypocrite*, a word in Greek that only Jesus speaks in Scripture. Scholar H. L. Ellison notes that in New Testament times, this word could be broadly understood as someone who was an actor, pretending to convince themselves of their right opinion or position on a matter.[8] Ellison says, "The judgment Jesus is particularly condemning is our efforts to make all conform to our own standards of perfection."[9] With that context, Jesus' words reach my ears like a blaring, urgent alarm:

"Do you have the nerve to say, 'Let me wash your face for you,' when your own face is distorted by contempt? . . . Wipe that ugly sneer off your own face, and you might be fit to offer a washcloth to your neighbor."[10]

In other words, I shouldn't criticize someone else's attempt to cross Little Colorado River Gorge while lying on my sofa, repeatedly hitting "snooze."

Some may have the nerve, but they don't have a washcloth for their own face.

Testing the Pillar: Self-Discipline

1. What are the "alarms" in your life or in the world that have captured your attention? Which ones have you chosen to respond to with your voice? Which have you ignored? Why?

2. Why do you think Nik Wallenda didn't need to practice at the Grand Canyon? How does that short narrative translate to the idea of self-discipline and accountability?

3. What commitments might you make to help bring accountability to how you use your voice? These questions can help you find your way:

   How would you like to show up in relationship with others?

   What do you want to be consistently true about your character and integrity?

What are boundaries in your behavior or in how you lend your voice that you're *not* willing to cross?

Who will you invite to hold those commitments with you, to remind you why they're important?

What, if anything, has prevented you from being open to holding yourself accountable? What resistance do you have to this pillar as a whole?

What, in your opinion, makes discipline something to celebrate?

CHAPTER 7

FROZEN IN TIME

[on initiative]

My kid walks through the back door after school and greets me with the widest smile.

"Did you get her?" I ask.

"Mom. I got her."

She came home from school last week not just excited but *eager* to work on her very first research project. This project will take weeks of planning and coordination, culminating in a full-on evening presentation at the school where students dress up as their characters and recite memorized speeches to passersby. It's a big deal.

But to start the project, you have to pick your person. This person has to be an author or poet you'll enjoy learning about, someone dead or alive who left a mark on literary history. Appropriately, the project is entitled "Frozen in Time." But there was a heightened tension built in: You had to list your top *two* authors in the event someone in your class wanted to research the same person.

My kid had gone to school today with nerves on edge. She knew who she wanted her person to be. But what if someone else picked that author too?

Now, squealing, homegirl runs up to her room, plucks her selection card out of her backpack, and pastes it on her wall.

In big letters, it reads: "ZORA NEALE HURSTON."

She's proud, and so am I.

A couple of weeks later, after she's finished the first few rounds of research and crafted a draft of her speech, I park to pick up the kids and notice her classmates carrying white poster boards out with them.

Today must be the day, I think.

As I walk toward her class, her teacher catches my eye. "You don't have to do it all tonight," she assures me.

I chuckle and mouth, "Thanks!"

The pressure to put together a picture-perfect poster immediately is off. I won't have to scramble to replace dried-out glue sticks, find paint-coated craft scissors, sharpen pencils, or cut construction paper. There won't be a need for the inevitable late-night hunt for printer ink. I can relax and enjoy our Friday night.

But that's not how the evening goes.

As soon as we get home, my kid is rushing around the house, collecting all the necessary supplies—glue, colored pencils, paper, markers—and I realize what is taking place.

"Wait, you're going to do your project now?"

"Yeah."

"Without my help?"

"Yup."

I don't know what to think. I'm stuck somewhere between feeling touched by the purity of her eagerness—and, well, developing hives. Because I know my kid. I also know what her room looks like.

She's got an artist's brain like her father's: free, wild, and wonderfully creative.

I take a deep breath, channel my inner Janet Lansbury parenting guru, and leave her to her work.

In that moment, I had to decide whether her drive and initiative were going to be more or less important than my stringent, adult expectations of not just what this project would become and what it would look like—but when it would happen.

I decided to let her initiative lead.

Riding the Tide

On July 8, 1876, as part of the American Centennial celebration, twenty-three-year-old Maria Spelterini completed a high-wire walk over the Niagara Gorge. She was the first and only woman to ever do so. While I imagine some spectators were wowed merely by the feat, undoubtedly others were impressed that this was, indeed, a woman who'd taken to the steel wire.

But that milestone wasn't enough for Maria. Something continued to drive her. Just four days later, on July 12, Maria was back on the wire—this time with peach baskets on her feet.

But she didn't stop there.

A week later, on July 19, Maria was back at it again. She successfully completed the same exact walk, but now with a paper bag over her head.

Wasn't that sufficient for her? With all the risks and potential for disaster, couldn't that first, second, third time be considered the pinnacle of accomplishment?

But on July 22 she showed up to the wire for a *fourth* time, this time wearing the most literal and metaphorically restrictive obstacle: ankles and wrist shackled in steel.

And on her fifth and final time across the Gorge in just nineteen days, Maria walked backwards, blind to what was behind her, yet driven and confident. Partway through, she decided to close the curtain on her multiday performance not by walking, but by dancing and skipping to the other side.[1]

Why did she do all this? What was the significance of these walks of escalating difficulty? What compelled her to struggle through, to prove to herself that she could break through and conquer?

In Shakespeare's *The Tragedy of Julius Caesar*, Roman general Marcus Brutus says to his friend Cassius,

> There is a tide in the affairs of men,
> Which, taken at the flood, leads on to fortune;
> Omitted, all the voyage of their life
> Is bound in shallows and in miseries.
> On such a full sea are we now afloat;
> And we must take the current when it serves,
> Or lose our ventures.[2]

Life brings with it an uncontrollable tide, circumstances that no human can direct. But sometimes those circumstances create opportunity. When we see those opportunities and do nothing, we stay stuck in the shallows. But when we choose to ride the tide, we're on our way somewhere.

Sometimes, opportunity comes in the form of art supplies and time at the kitchen table after school. Sometimes it's a wire that wasn't immediately taken down after a successful first walk. Riding the tide of opportunity requires an internal, self-propelled drive.

As we steward the voices we have been given, we have to consider the opportunities our souls naturally gravitate toward, the ones where no one has to prod or convince or convict us to speak. In those opportunities where both our passion and natural "yes" propel us forward, even if the final destination is unknown, we should give full heart and attention.

Maybe you find yourself coming home after work still thinking about that community engagement project, or every year you don't mind giving extra energy to rallying your family around a service opportunity at the food bank. Perhaps you go out of your way to support local farmers and food growers, or you're happy to sacrifice time in your schedule to mentor a high school student from a different part of your city.

You've decided to ride the tide at flood stage.

Find the opportunities you're driven to meet. Those will continue to be the places that can hold you accountable not just for your time but for the fullness of what you value and believe.

Find the places where you are undeterred by potential risks or difficulties. Notice where you're not concerned about the opinions of spectators who are there one day and then gone the next. Place your voice and your presence where initiative naturally flares to life.

Initiative doesn't show up in the same way and the same spaces for everyone. Some may never be driven to decrease violence in the city or carry the banner for women to be represented equally and enthusiastically in the workplace. This may not be because they don't see the value. It may just be because they're riding a different tide.

All that really matters is that you discern and decide which tide to take. Take the tide at the flood. Then you can grab the map, test the wind, and read the stars along the way.

The Risk of Initiative

Years ago I was one of few people of color in a meeting when someone asked how we would achieve visible and public racial representation as part of that particular project. I could feel my throat tighten. While I was glad someone (other than me) was looking through lenses that impacted all the people we were trying to include, empower, and serve, I knew what often came next in a room where I'd be seen as a voice for the "visible and public racial representation." I didn't want to be put on the spot as a token or "expert" in the proverbial field of Blackness, which meant I would need to thread a difficult needle, both stating what was true of my own experience and refusing to speak for every person henceforth and forevermore who identifies as Black.

Out of the corner of my eye, I noticed my friend scribbling a note in my planner. Her words were simple: *This isn't on you.* She wanted me to know that the pressure was off, that I wasn't solely responsible for carrying the weight of that conversation. I could (and did) participate, but she reminded me that I was free from the expectation to single-handedly solve the tension of the topic. That expectation was far from my burden to bear alone.

We have to pause here and acknowledge an uncomfortable truth: Sometimes our initiative will press into lives and wounds we are unaware of. When we steward our voices in the context of communal interdependence, we will meet the sometimes untold and unnamed stories of the people around us. This is both a risk and an opportunity for humility and growth. We must pay attention to the impact of our initiative, being aware of the gaps in our understanding so we can, with wisdom and compassion, be attuned to other hearts on the journey.

I'm sure the leader of the meeting didn't know my throat would tighten at the mention of racial representation. I was literally a leader at the table, one who'd been invited and asked to lend my perspective. Everyone in that room, including me, was there to help. Thankfully, there was at least one person in attendance who knew me well enough to anticipate how that particular request for help would meet my ears and heart. I was at the table—but I was also known.

Our initiative cannot be devoid of emotional intelligence. Nor can our initiative degenerate into a lazy passivity where we outsource our pursuit of knowledge or awareness. If our initiative looks only like asking and expecting others to share of themselves or their experiences (some of which may come at the great cost of reliving pain or even traumatic episodes), involving little to none of our own emotional or temporal labor; if we ask others to bear heavy burdens because bearing them ourselves is inconvenient; if we don't look for and consider other resources we could learn from, resources that don't require other human beings to sacrifice for our growth—then our initiative undermines the inherent mutuality required for the work of navigating canyons of difference.

We mentioned a couple of ways to get at this earlier, our own research of primary resources being one. But try driving through and investing money and time in parts of your city that others would consider less developed. Buy from small-business owners and attend events at a public park or local library. Attend open lectures at local schools and universities. Pick up a hobby that puts you in regular proximity to people whose perspectives you desire to learn from.

The reality we all walk through is that history has unfairly impacted generations of Indigenous American people groups and people of color (like some of my ancestors, who weren't free to own land until after the transatlantic slave trade was abolished and slaves were freed). Injustice has prevented some from being able to accumulate wealth quickly or at all and prevented others from having access to top-tier educational institutions, healthy food options (due to transportation limitations), or secure housing (due to job options or income status).

It's inhospitable to ask everything of someone from whom so much has already been taken. Even if you didn't know. Even if they choose not to let you in. Hospitality welcomes in and offers "home" to others. Placing additional burdens on those who have historically fought for justice and equity, or who've even just lived in the tension of these realities, offers not "home" but more hard work. It offers not a safe space to be seen and nourished but additional demand and strain.

This is the risk of initiative. You may enter sincerely curious, eager to know more. You may make the ask, and the response may be *no* or *not yet*. You may not even get a verbal response but instead find yourself encountering emotions as big as the waves upon which you've set sail. When we step into initiative, we are responsible for how our initiative lands. Someone else isn't "wrong" or "too sensitive" or "unable to understand what we're trying to accomplish." Intentions matter, and those intentions must explicitly extend to honoring and making right the places where our intentions can cause—or have caused—harm.

This caution and subsequent tenderness certainly apply to race. In one column, a Black correspondent and editor explains a portion of her experience:

Asking black people in the United States to discuss race is asking them to relive every moment of pain, fear, and outrage they have experienced: the insult of a supervisor who objected to your going to China to report but was very open to sending you to Africa, or the distress of having your child picked up by the police . . . because he "looked like someone." . . . Too often the white friends who want their black friends to educate them about race don't do that work, and don't accept that being uncomfortable with black anger is part of that work.[3]

In any area of division, initiative looks like doing the work and then being willing to be uncomfortable. If you're seeking to understand race in America and then using your own voice to expose and alleviate historical injustices: work and willingness. If you're striving to understand the experience of Indigenous peoples: work and willingness. If you're advocating for *imago Dei* to be upheld in the lives and stories of the LGBTQ community: work and willingness. If you're trying to navigate pro-life/pro-choice debates in a way that rejects unnuanced binaries: work and willingness.

We cannot truly do the work without the willingness to adapt and grow, no matter how difficult that is or how uncomfortable we feel. That's why our voices and desires to say good are a stewardship. They stretch and impact far beyond the reach of our own place in the world.

The Accountability of Initiative

The town is Capernaum, a fishing village on the northern shore of the Sea of Galilee. Word has gotten around: Jesus is here. People flock to where they hear he is preaching. Disciples and skeptics alike stand shoulder-to-shoulder, listening in to what he has to say.

If you came late, you're not getting in. There's not even "standing room only," inside or out. To say a crowd has accumulated would be an understatement. If you don't like who you're standing next to, tough. You aren't leaving, and no one is going to be able to make their way past you.

Somewhere, a considerable distance away, is a paralyzed man. He probably heard the word too but knows he won't be able to get to the home where Jesus is as quickly as everyone else can. But all is not lost. Four men—friends who offer to give him a lift, perhaps four seemingly random people who agree to help him—carry him to the house where Jesus is.

Walking up to the house where Jesus is preaching, they see the overflow of bodies, people craning their necks and hoisting kids on shoulders in hopes of catching a glimpse. That's when they rule out the crowded doorway and instead take the initiative to get creative.

They see an obstacle, but they also see the tide of opportunity in the shape of a roof.

And so they climb and carry, risking a slipped foot or an unsteady hand. As they strain and sweat, they hear Jesus' muffled words. Their hearts beating faster, they know how awkward this is about to be. They haven't mapped this out or come up with a more put-together plan, but they aren't turning back now. They start digging.

Neighbors and those inside the house surely start noticing the falling debris, the disturbance above them. Jesus looks up, pausing to get a glimpse of the light breaking through and the shadows beyond it.

And then a figure overhead, descending.

Some in the crowd are shocked because of the absurdity of it all. They know these five men and are embarrassed. In their culture of honor and shame, this whole episode reflects negatively on their families. Some kids are giggling; parents, aunts, and uncles shoot them stern looks.

But then, finally, the paralyzed man is with Jesus.

With a crowd of people watching, these five men have risked everything on behalf of one man. They've mustered the discipline to coordinate and work together. They've put in the work, willing to be uncomfortable before their community and the One they are all there to see. No matter what happens next, they can't hide. The damage has been done.[4]

Whenever we take initiative, however we risk our way forward, we're going to be accountable for what follows.

If we choose to step foot toward hope—whether that hope comes in the form of proximity to healing or the realization of repair in other broken places—our initiative may also mean we're owning what lies in the wake of those steps we take. These men must've known they were going to damage someone else's roof. I bet they were already willing and prepared to take accountability for it. They'd decided that the hope of seeing their friend changed by Jesus was worth it.

Mark's Gospel notes that Jesus took note of *their faith*, not their audacity or creativity. He says to the paralyzed man, "Son, your sins are forgiven."[5]

I imagine the paralyzed stranger turning in shock. *Son?*

The teachers of the law are outraged.

And so Jesus turns his attention to the ones too stubborn to see and puts his authority on display. He tells the paralyzed man to get up, take his mat, and go home. And the man does.

The crowd must've parted because their original entrance is his mic-drop exit. The text says he walked out "in full view of them all."[6] Now, the miracle performed after his friends' initiative is his gift to steward. He is accountable, not just to the action taken by his friends (he was, after all, supposedly willing and involved) but also to what he does with the outcome, the miracle on the other side.

Some might say that taking initiative in this way—putting in the work, being willing to be made uncomfortable, and taking ownership of whatever follows—might look a lot like faith.

Accountability keeps us in community, and it keeps us honest, not just to our actions but also to stewarding the breakthrough on the other side.

The first poster was *very* abstract—and not what I would've chosen. Zora Neale Hurston's name was not centered along the long edge of the poster board. There was a visiting snowflake stencil drawn onto the lower right-hand corner.

The initiative had produced something wildly different than I expected, but she'd put in the work. With the freedom of her imagination and the motivation inside her, she'd produced something she was proud of.

Without wanting to hurt her feelings, I asked her if she wanted to make two posters and then decide which one she felt fit the brief for the project. In the seconds where she stood there considering the suggestion, I felt like Maria Spelterini at the edge of Niagara Falls. Would this one comment turn into tears? Would there be a definitive no? I'd given her the option.

To my surprise, she thought this was a great idea.

And so the pressure was on: scrambling to replace dried-out glue sticks and find paint-coated craft scissors; printing everything she needed over again (except without any ink emergencies, thank God). I sharpened pencils, she brought the construction paper back out, and she cut and glued and drew.

Her initiative led, and together, we worked. She was accountable to a teacher's ask, and I was accountable to her—to let go of all the control I wanted to wield, the one-sided burden I so badly wanted to place on her shoulders in the shape of a mother's unfair expectations.

We worked.

We took the tide at the flood without having all the answers, refusing to stay frozen in time. And in the end, after every fact was glued and every picture was secured, the poster was hers. It was up to her to steward that work into the world.

Testing the Pillar: Initiative

1. What recent opportunities have you given yourself to with abandon, throwing yourself into the tide? What did these opportunities have in common? Write down any common threads you might have noticed. How might those threads help inform what you lend your voice, time, and creativity to in the future?

2. Conversely, can you think of times you decided against an opportunity to speak or lend your voice? Why? What do you notice about the circumstances surrounding those situations? What might your decisions in those moments teach you? Which ones would you say no to again? Which ones were places where you needed more courage?

3. When has taking initiative landed you "in a field of trouble you didn't know was being harvested"? Who were the people involved, and how did you respond? Was there anything you'd do differently?

4. How would you define *initiative*? What changes when you view initiative through the lenses of work and willingness?

5. What stood out to you about the story of Jesus and the paralyzed man from Mark 2:1-12?

CHAPTER 8

FIX YOUR FACE

[on hard truth]

I'm about to graduate from my master's program, and I have one question I want to ask the dean of the School of Leadership and Business before I leave. I've thought about this question and turned it over carefully, wordsmithing it just so. I want him to see a student intentionally seeking feedback, not carelessly wasting his time.

As I take a seat in the dean's office, I start by expressing my gratitude for his wisdom and guidance. He's truly been one of my most refreshingly encouraging and sharp-shooting mentors: no fluff, but no unnecessary jabs either. This man masterfully displays what truth and grace look like in the context of leadership.

Now, to ask him my question.

"This won't take long," I promise, "but as I graduate, and as you consider what you've observed of my leadership skills over the past few months, I have just one question: What, from your perspective, would be one thing I could do to help me become a more effective leader?"

Scrunching my forehead to draw him into focus, I look at him across his desk, proud of my poise and delivery.

He smiles under his full beard and mustache and gives a short huff.

"You really want to know?" he asks.

"Yes," I tell him. "I really want to know."

The next seconds feel like an eternity.

Someone You Can Trust

We can project our voices into a lot of conflict and division, but nothing we say will have an impact—except maybe a negative one—if we're not speaking from a place of trust. Trust is foundational to accountability, which may be why we have an accountability problem here in the United States. As recently as July 2019, the Pew Research Center rolled out a new study on trust and distrust in America, examining how Americans see problems of trust; the state of personal trust; and Americans' struggles with trust, accuracy, and accountability.[1]

The report revealed that an alarming percentage of Americans did not trust their fellow citizens. Of those polled, 71 percent "think that interpersonal trust has declined" in the past twenty years, with various reasons cited for the decline, including:

- "social and policy woes"

- "the nation's continuing struggles with race relations, crime, and religion versus secularism"

- "others' personal traits such as laziness, greed, and dishonesty"

- "toxic national politics and polarization"[2]

So our interpersonal confidence problem has worsened—and some of the reasons why are among our biggest points of disagreement and division. How can we build trust again to start addressing these divides?

We've got to start with becoming trustworthy. And part of becoming worthy of trust is facing where we aren't. The problem is, those places where our trustworthiness erodes are often our blind spots. That's where accountability enters in. Who are we willing to receive feedback from? Who is discerning and courageous enough to help us pay attention to areas we can't yet see but which may be the greatest barriers to people trusting *us*?

I've asked coworkers to let me know if I'm walking around with proverbial "broccoli in my teeth." Think of it this way: If someone tries to tell me I have literal broccoli in my teeth, I can choose to receive or reject that feedback. But if I choose to reject it, not only do I risk walking around looking like a hot-mess express, chances are high that person will be less likely to do me a solid should it happen again. Similarly, I want people to tell me if something about my words or approach has a negative impact on the flourishing of others, impacting their ability to trust me as a leader—and I want to get that broccoli out of my teeth.

People who listen and learn from hard truth are people who build trust. If we refuse to hear the most unintentional ways we might ding or even fully sever trust, if literally *no one* has the influence in our lives to lovingly reveal things about us we cannot see, then that's where our work should start—not with popular hot takes but by going deep beneath our resistance to hearing the truth about ourselves.

Even if we see the value in receiving hard truth, we can't avoid a significant barrier we're going to encounter: that often other people resist offering it, particularly when power dynamics are at play.

It all boils down to this: Giving and receiving hard truth is, well, hard.

But if someone is willing to give it, we're on the hook for how we receive it. We're responsible to discern how much of it we hold as a gift, what parts help us live as more redeemed versions of ourselves.

All that assumes, of course, that we can trust each other in the first place. As we seek to more thoughtfully engage with high-tension areas—whether personal, organizational, or communal—we have to consider our own relationship with hard truth: what it looks like to receive it, what it looks like to give it, and who we trust enough that we'll listen to it.

How to Receive

In Mark 10, we meet a man who's quite rich—some might say he has everything. I imagine him living the high life, maybe kickin' it with Beyoncé, Oprah, or Jeff Bezos on a yacht somewhere in the Maldives—certainly not kneeling before someone else in a posture of surrender and submission. But that's where this guy surprises me: He kneels before Jesus.

This tells me something important about how he relates to Jesus. Kneeling was, in the first century as it is today, a sign of respect.

Then this man addresses Jesus a very specific way: "Good teacher." With his question—"What must I do to inherit eternal life?"[3]—we see that he's spiritually sensitive, longing for something his money can't buy him. Calling Jesus "good" has implications. In the first century, it was understood that God alone was perfectly good. Did this man believe something deeper about Jesus than Jesus had even revealed about himself? At the very least, theologians assume the man thought Jesus knew something, not just about the material world but about how to take hold of eternal life.[4]

As good teachers often do, Jesus replies to the man's question with a question. (How frustrating, right? I don't ask questions to be asked questions. Just give me the answer!) This man has identified Jesus as a teacher, even a good one, but Jesus knows he's still missing a key piece: Unless this guy recognizes him not just as a teacher, but as God, eternal life will yet be out of reach. That's the rich man's first whoopsie.

And here's the second: This guy, likely used to being able to buy his way into or out of most things, assumes he can just as easily attain the life he's so desperately seeking. He tells Jesus how he's kept the commandments since he was a young boy. Surely his education, piety, and money are enough for what he wants.

But then, before we get to Jesus' response, we read one important detail:

And Jesus, looking at him, loved him.[5]

Before telling the rich guy what he lacked, Jesus looked at him. Before he let the rich man know what eternal life would truly cost, he loved him. Something Jesus saw in this man stirred his affections for him, drawing him to *agape* love. *Agape* love is the most transcendent kind of love possible: from God the Father to humanity, and from humanity back to God. And *agape* "extends to the love of one's fellow humans, as the reciprocal love between God and humans is made manifest in one's unselfish love of others."[6]

Do you see it? Jesus' first response to this man's lack, his opening posture before speaking a hard truth, was an unselfish and transcendent love. Distrust didn't clog the gap; neither did judgment or harshness or a grossly satisfying kind of disdain.

This kneeling man clearly trusted Jesus to provide the answer he was so longing for. And Jesus, in turn, didn't betray that trust. Instead, he modeled what it looks like to tether trust to love, only then extending into the truth he likely knew would be so hard for this rich young ruler to hear:

> "You lack one thing: go, sell all that you have and give to the poor, and you will have treasure in heaven; and come, follow me."[7]

Religious teachers would often test the wealthy person's commitment to their teachings by asking them to greatly sacrifice their wealth. In Judaism, charitable giving was highly valued, but Jesus—a good teacher indeed—isn't interested in simply testing whether this man does the "right things" with money. Jesus is going deeper, right to this man's motivations. Jesus is going after his heart.

I can see that man looking into Jesus' face, witnessing and absorbing and feeling undeniable love—but now hearing how his heart and hands must be pried away from the things he's held on to so tightly. As Jesus speaks, I imagine this man's brow furrowing, the pit of his stomach tightening as he pictures his lavish life and all that it has meant for him socially slipping away: the food, the clothes, the status, and the prestige. It's too painful, too much. How could selling everything he has and giving it to the less esteemed somehow compute to greater treasure than his current hoard?

The hard truth hits. There's broccoli in his teeth, something stuck and in the way. It's his money, what he has. He surely knows it now. He knows—and it's too much.

Here's where we need to lean in. We might be tempted to focus solely on the rich young ruler as an example of what *not* to do. For those of us who follow Jesus and long to be formed into his likeness, we're likely going, "Give it up, man! Just do the hard thing!"

But I actually think this man shows us how it looks to receive hard truth well. He trusts Jesus, even physically positioning himself in such a way as to communicate profound respect. He listens, hears Jesus out, and walks away with new information. He hears the hard truth well; he just chooses not to heed it.

Let's break down some of the key things we can learn from the rich man about how to receive hard truth:

- **Know who you trust.** We need to examine our trust level before we decide to ask for hard truth. If there's little to no trust, we won't be able posture ourselves in a respectful way and may need to consider forgoing that conversation. If the hard truth is unsolicited, we'll have to work harder to engage the part of us that can graciously hear without needing to heed.

- **Have the right posture.** Our physical posture matters. Crossed arms and rolled eyes communicate something, and it ain't usually respect. (This one's tough for me. I'm notorious for crossing my arms when I'm cold—and I'm *always* cold.) How we choose to sit, stand, or slump sends a message. How would you receive a gift, even one you didn't ask for? Our posture can make all the difference in how the giver chooses to share and how the interaction ends. (If you're not receiving feedback in person, I encourage you to reconsider your approach. Nonverbal cues can make or break a conversation, and in an increasingly disconnected-yet-connected age, in-person proximity is rare and rich.)

- **Listen well.** It's okay to honestly evaluate whether we're in a place and space to listen well. I cannot handle hard conversations while I'm making school lunches and kids are sneaking Girl Scout cookies out of the pantry or while I'm doing science experiments with baking soda and chemicals. Even if it's helpful feedback, I won't hear it then, and not because I wouldn't want to. My capacity needs to be cleared, like a countertop. Too many inputs cluttering the counter and there's hardly space for anything else, especially the implications of a hard conversation.

How to Give

The rich young ruler did a lot of things well when it came to receiving hard truth. But if we're going to steward our voices in the middle of tensions and complexities, if we're going to stick our opinions and wisdom and experiences into spaces where change is possible and decisions are made, we need to learn to give hard truth as well. And for that, we have to shift our focus to Jesus as the giver.

Humility in the work of giving hard truth is a prerequisite. We can never be Jesus and should be careful not to insert ourselves *as* him as we seek to live *like* him. But part of learning to talk tightropes is being willing to learn and grow and be transformed over time until our words, motivations, and actions look more and more like Jesus' own.

Here are some things we can learn from Jesus about giving hard truths:

- **Discern the relationship.** The first thing Jesus does is clarify the relationship between him and the rich man. Why is this man calling him good? Does he see Jesus just as a source of basic wisdom and knowledge? Or does he recognize Jesus as someone walking more in the fullness of his nature as God?

  As givers of hard truth, we must consider our relationship to those on the other side of the proverbial table. Does a relationship exist at all? And if so, in what context has this relationship existed before we arrived at this conversation? Have there been years' worth of hard truths exchanged regularly, mutually, and in a spirit of love and grace? Or is this the first time approaching hard truth with this person? Is this a family member you see every day? Or a distant friend you haven't seen since college all those years ago? While relationships have the potential to get stronger *because* we're willing to lean into the hard things in a healthy way, we should intentionally take stock of relational markers like power dynamics, whether there is a past history of mutuality, and what we actually envision or hope for this relationship going forward. Do we sincerely want the best for this person? If they failed in achieving a goal that meant a lot to them—or were on the receiving end of dire misfortune—would we notice, care, or even celebrate?

- **Leave room for response.** The next thing Jesus does is subtle but important. He creates space for the rich man to respond. When I'm preparing to deliver a message of any kind, whether during a conversation or more formally before a crowd, I care a lot—almost exclusively, I admit—about what I'm going to say. Most of the time this instinct comes from a pure place. Intentionality and delivery matter. But Jesus gives us an important reminder to pause. Before blazing ahead to the summit of his answer, Jesus leaves enough space for this man to respond, to verbally process his understanding up to that point.

Do you think we could use more of this in our cultural moment? I sincerely wonder if a lot of the polarization and negative perceptions we have of each other come down to us refusing to leave room. We're more interested in what we have to say than in how our words meet another's ears; more interested in our position than in how that position may stir hearts and minds. Trust cannot grow or expand if we refuse to give it room. Dialogue dies where it's suffocated.

- **Look and Love.** Before he exposes lack, Jesus looks and loves. This encounter is personal and intimate. Jesus sees the person, cares about his heart, and then delivers what is true.

  Oftentimes I'm guilty of dishing "hard truth" to not just one but to the masses. I wonder how this skews the way I look and love when the "who" is so severely blurred, when there's no face or actual life to imagine on the other side. So I ask these questions of myself as much as I'm asking you: When we give hard truths, are we looking before we lead with our voices? Are we seeing the other person's humanity before verbalizing what we long to say? Does our love propel us to proceed with care? Would the other person be able to tell we are moved on their behalf?

When profound grace is tied to love, clear truth won't shy away—and only then does it have the chance to create good, lasting change.

Fix Your Face

"You really want to know?" asks the dean.

"Yes," I tell him. "I really want to know."

Those short yet pregnant seconds as he pauses feel unbearable.

"Fix your face," he says shortly. The three words come out clear as day, but not with malice or an adversarial edge.

I feel my eyebrows shoot up as if they're trying to escape through the ceiling.

"Excuse me?" I ask. I'm not offended, but I *am* desperately craving an explanation. Over the course of months, this man has proven his investment in me and the rest of my cohort. He's taught us and steered us and advocated for us. He's the dean of the School of Leadership for a reason, and I came to him wanting truth.

With a soft smile, he looks directly into my eyes and continues: "Ashlee, you have one of the most expressive faces I've come across. It helps communicate your vulnerability and authenticity. It works to your advantage—until it doesn't. There are times when your facial expressions will deter from what you mean to communicate, or when they won't be helpful or appropriate in response to something you disagree with. You'll need to lead anyway. And in order to lead anyway, you'll need to fix your face."

I can feel the bottom half of my jaw hanging open, and slowly coax it back up so that my lips meet in a straight line. I'm floored, but not because I'm hurt by what he's shared. I'm more shocked, I realize, by the fact that he cares for me enough to actually share feedback he knows could potentially be hard for me to receive.

More than that, the dean hasn't shared some pithy, generic leadership advice like "Follow your heart!" or "Just keep going!" or "Practice your power stance!" His hard truth communicates he's been watching me, observing how I learn and engage with others. He's been studying me, as good leaders do. And I realize something: This is what it means to be looked at with *agape* love, unselfish in its pursuit of another's flourishing. The dean didn't have to be so honest. He could've copped out, and I would've been none the wiser.

To this day, I've never forgotten those three words. I also still have the book he recommended I read, a practical next step to follow his hard truth. That book is appropriately titled *The Definitive Book of Body Language: The Hidden Meaning behind People's Gestures and Expressions.*

I'm still pretty readable when it comes to my facial expressions. If I'm enjoying myself, you'll know. And if I'm anxious, disappointed, annoyed, or sad—it's usually not hard to tell. I'm a work in progress, always. But those words and how they came to me all those years ago help hold me accountable to this day, and I'm decidedly better for them.

In the continued work of becoming both good givers and good receivers of hard truth, I hope you'll fix your face, and not just on the message you feel entrusted to carry forward or the conviction burning strong in your heart; I hope you'll fix your face on the people waiting for you on the other side of what you have to say. I hope you'll choose to look at and love them well, that you'll love before you unleash. That you'll say no if true trust isn't there, that you'll wait until you *want* them to thrive. I hope you'll wait with eager ears to be blessed by good truth. I hope you'll choose to listen without defense yet full of confidence, that you'll accept what is given and said in trust, and that you'll graciously reject what isn't.

Fix your face on the ones who will cheer you across, no matter how hard the truth.

Testing the Pillar: Hard Truth

1. *Do you really want to know?* is a question that tests your willingness to receive hard truth. What circumstances or conditions make you less likely to want to know?

2. Do you agree with the Pew Research Center's reasons for decline in interpersonal confidence? What strategies or changes in interpersonal confidence and trust-building do you imagine might reverse the decline? What is one commitment you can make when handling hard truth (either as a giver or receiver) that can be part of the solution?

3. What's one takeaway you'd like to further reflect on in the story of Jesus and the rich young ruler? What new insight can you turn into an action step?

4. Think of a recent situation where you needed to receive hard truth. Looking back, what would you have changed about your posture?

5. Now think of a time when you needed to deliver hard truth. What would you have changed about your delivery? In future interactions, what would change if you more intentionally looked at and loved people?

6. Thank someone who's shared hard truth with you. Express your gratitude for their risk and investment in your flourishing.

PART IV

Influence

*Let us think of ways to motivate one another
to acts of love and good works.*

HEBREWS 10:24, NLT

*The most common way people give up their
power is by thinking they don't have any.*

ALICE WALKER

The PAIR Pillars

Passion
Accountability
Influence
Relationship

As you consider the first two pillars of passion and accountability and how they might be directing you to use your voice to say good, you may find yourself asking something like "If I don't have thousands of followers on social media, what's the point, anyway?" Or perhaps you're one who could care less about social media. Here's the point: Social media isn't the sole—or even the most significant—marker of influence. Every single person, including you, has a place where their voice holds weight: a city, a neighborhood, an office building; a favorite park, a kitchen table, a gym. Everyone has places where their voice and presence matter, where someone might be leaning in to absorb and appreciate what they think. We all have the ability to show up and wield influence in places we've been asked to steward well, regardless of how widely known those places are.

Jesus made the most of a journey to a well. He created teachable moments around meals and wowed guests at a wedding. For Jesus, present places were prime opportunities. We need not look far—or to the wildly changing, algorithm-driven chaos of digital affirmation—for our voices to make a real difference. We shouldn't wait until it seems we've attracted a crowd. Leverage where you are, right now. That is the steadying pillar of influence.

CHAPTER 9

"SEARCH MAPS"

[on place + space]

The little blue dot in my phone's Maps app fascinates me, because it tells me exactly where I am at any given time. That one dot orients me to everything around me—I can select "Search Maps" and figure out how to get anywhere I want. Coffee shop nearby? "Search maps." Boba tea? "Search maps."

Sometimes I zoom in close on that blue dot, and then I take my pointer and thumb fingers pinching, pinching, zooming back out until I can see the block, then the neighborhood, then the town, then the city. I keep going until I can see the state I'm in, then the country, then the continent. Zooming all the way out gets me to a 3D rendition of the Earth with tiny pixel pricks for stars. As I spin the entire world beneath the swirls of my fingerprint, I think of all the pain and beauty and conflict within its oceans and islands and green swatches of land. Things may be quiet where I sit, but at the same time, war wages between Russia and Ukraine; kids build friendships on a playground not so far away; a mother fights for custody of her kids in a downtown city hall. Farmers plant new seeds; a family gathers to make arrangements for their son who was lost to gang violence; a couple poses for pictures with their long-prayed-for newborn baby.

On one hand, I am in awe of how all our lives crash and slide past one another, like neon-bright bubbles floating up and down in a lava lamp. On the other, I'm overwhelmed: There's just so much to care about. How do I hold all the pain and beauty and conflict that this world screams through the headlines?

It's too much.

Too much is the reason I say nothing, covertly scrolling past other people's posts and protests from under my duvet.

Too much is the reason I type with abandon, fingers tripping over fingers trying to capture the overflow of thoughts.

My voice is not enough to hold it all. Or perhaps my voice is too much. I should move on, care about something else.

I take my thumb and swipe until I'm back, hovering over North America and that little blue dot. It reminds me that I haven't moved, even though I've moved the world and all its cares with a touch. Though my mind has wandered and my heart has pounded prayers in the world's direction, that little blue dot calls me home. *YOU ARE HERE*, it reminds me.

My pointer and thumb fingers spread apart across the screen now, bringing me closer: The world is now the country is now the state is now the street. The blue dot blinks. *Don't go far*, it seems to say. *Start here.*

The Choice to Stay

The circle suddenly seems so small.

The heat pools around us in this room of concrete and white walls and patched ceiling tiles. On one side of the seated circle sit neighbors from a small sector just about two hours outside Kigali, Rwanda, a tapestry of bright colors and patterned dresses. On the other side of the circle is a tapestry of a different kind: various melanated skin tones across thirteen pastors and nonprofit leaders visiting from the United States.

Just a day earlier, we soberly made our way through the Kigali Genocide Memorial, reading notes of gut-wrenching longing and loving last words alongside family photos of loved ones-turned-victims of the horrific 1994 Rwandan genocide. From April 7, 1994, to July 15, 1994, mounting ethnic tensions erupted into a furious killing rampage. Though the genocide claimed victims from all Rwandan people groups, ethnic minority Tutsis were the target. In less than three months, the death toll reached almost a million people.[1]

As we absorbed the history through museum installations and story, I tried not to vomit, and not just because of the countless pedestrian images of bodies in the streets, some covered, some exposed to the elements and the indignity of such a heinous end. No—what sickened me was that this was all true. This was all real, recent history, once just a Monday or a Tuesday in my very young life. I was swinging innocently on the swing set of my all-girls' Catholic school in Houston, Texas, while on the other side of the world, neighbors killed neighbors with the swing of a machete.

And now here we are, just over twenty-five years later, submitting ourselves to that history. We are a group of spiritual leaders and guides, but our goal this day is to humbly learn from a country's tragedy and triumph, that the sins of some may not be repeated in our context. Not on our watch. Not when we hear of pastors during the genocide either refusing to say a thing to condemn the atrocities—or even actively participating in the killing, locking congregants inside to be extinguished en masse.

We walked the grounds of the memorial, monstrous slabs of stone atop some 250,000 bodies in mass graves. Now we are here, outside the city, to witness the work that followed—after the last human being was killed, after the Rwandan Patriotic Front, led by the Tutsi-dominated rebel movement, captured Kigali. Over ten thousand people were eventually tried in Rwandan national courts for genocide-related crimes.

But the scope of harm was so much larger than those courts could handle. In 2002, a community justice system called *gacaca* (pronounced ga-CHA-cha) was established with the goal to "deliver justice and punish perpetrators while restoring the fabric of society."[2]

Under *gacaca*, locally elected judges heard the testimonies of witnesses, survivors, and perpetrators. Defendants were given the opportunity to confess and ask for forgiveness, and they received lower sentences if they were repentant and sincerely pursued reconciliation in their community. Victims were given a chance to forgive. Over the course of seven years, the *gacaca* court systems tried 1.2 million cases.[3]

We are now sitting before men and women who knew that court system well, most as survivors or witnesses but some as perpetrators.

The heat in the room thickens. Beads of sweat rise to the surface of my arms beneath my denim shirt, but I don't think it has anything to do with the temperature.

Eventually, a man and a woman stand up. Over the course of the next few minutes, time seems to move at the speed of held breath as, speaking side by side, they reveal their relational connection: The man had killed one of the woman's family members.

Stunned, we listen to the story. The woman hadn't known where her family member had been killed, making closure as part of her grieving process impossible. But the man, through the *gacaca* court process, had confessed he knew where her family member was buried—because he was responsible. After his confession, the man led her to the spot where he'd earned the label *murderer*.

But perhaps more shocking than the confession, more shocking than truth coming to light—was that the woman had offered this man forgiveness. They are able to stand here in this room, shoulder to shoulder, just a short distance from the neighborhood where they both now live. This new neighborhood wasn't built by an outsourced company or a band of well-meaning international volunteers. Rather, neighbors, together, built these homes. Neighbors formerly labeled by society as "helpless victim" or "heartless murderer." For all the high-level genocide cases outsourced to the International Criminal Tribunal for Rwanda, these people know and live this reality: There is significant, culture-changing work to do closer to home.

Originally, these neighborhoods were called reconciliation villages. Deo Gashagaza, a pastor and cofounder of a local Christian organization called Prison Fellowship Rwanda, helped come up with the idea as part of the nation's larger plan for healing. "Rebuilding the nation requires everyone to help," he said. "We still have a lot of things to do for our communities, for social cohesion. It's painful, but it's a journey of healing."[4]

How can this kind of healing actually take place? What makes it possible for murderers to confess, for witnesses and victims to forgive? How can someone, not far from painful wounds, still reliving recurring nightmares, live next door to the person responsible?

Out of our entire time in Rwanda, the cool balm of healing in that hot room is what I remember most. In our own country of America, we have increasingly become tangled up in divisions, in ethnic and racial tensions. We're pitted against one another politically, exposed to just how much we're willing to be against our neighbors, our friends, our families—over differences of opinion in policy, religion, and even the recollection and narrative of our history.

And in the middle of all this, I can't help but think of the church leaders during the Rwandan genocide: both the ones who were complicit and the ones who were absent in mind, body, and voice. And I wonder: Twenty-five years from now, what narrative will be written about me? About us?

At the end of the day, if you and I—as neighbors, pastors, family members, friends, or strangers—were to find ourselves as oppressors or victims, would we make the same choice to confess? Would we choose to forgive? Would we choose to stay with one another, moving our household goods and our hearts as close as one can get, right next door to the one who wears the face of our enemy or our prey? Would we sit around a circle together in the hope that a different testimony might come from the still-smoking ashes?

In the small Russian republic of Dagestan, virtually every able-bodied person learns to tightrope walk at a young age. Legend has it that the tradition stems from young men looking for more efficient ways to court women in neighboring mountainous regions. Yet other locals think that the practice has more to do with their harsh weather and hard winters—that when bridges broke in the elements, locals would instead cross to desired destinations by rope.

Today, the area is politically and economically unstable, draining training facilities of their usual funds. But the tightrope walkers who have stayed don't have to go far to walk into the legacy that has been left for them—and the broken places in their community that threaten that legacy.[5]

The choice to stay matters. In the fifth century, a monk named Benedict of Nursia had a vivid vision of community that helped carry the church through the crumbling of the Roman Empire. As part of his "Benedictine Rule," as this vision would come to be known, he established a vow of stability. Author Nathan Oates explains,

> The original and immediate meaning . . . was to live steadfastly in the monastery until death. The monastery was the workshop for the soul, and in order to get soul work done, one needed to stay in the workshop.[6]

Benedict defined *stability* not as having enough resources to exercise a sense of independence—but as a choice to stay. Even though Americans these days are less geographically mobile than before,[7] American history tells a tale of pursuit: pursuing land, pursuing fortune, pursuing a dream that would secure generations of prosperity and freedom. Now, this pursuit surely came at a cost, one of the most grievous being that Indigenous peoples suffered exploitation, exile, disease, and death as settlers pursued their lands. In our day, many generations-old Black, Latino, and immigrant communities are watching their cities and neighborhoods shift as developers pursue profit by buying homes and businesses out from under hardworking families. As family-owned storefronts turn in to your newest neighborhood Starbucks, whole communities can no longer pay to stay.

This long history of pursuit betrays a cultural reality: Americans like to move. We like to take flights to other states and countries to see sights and eat good food. We like to move in our cars and on city buses for work and entertainment. We like to move physically and—given key tech advancements like social media, videoconferencing applications like Zoom, and twenty-four-hour news services—we can now move emotionally. At the sound of a *ding*, our attention diverts to breaking news, the latest update in a key election, the hottest celebrity gossip, or charged headlines that pull on our heartstrings. With the touch of a button or the swipe of a thumb, we're transported to the most urgent cares of the media world—even if those cares aren't personally important to us.

In the midst of this chaos and the heavy demands on our time and our souls, what if part of stewarding our voices well is partaking in the modern-day version of Benedict's vow of stability?

It's not that we'll never move to a different neighborhood or to a different state for work. It's not that we can't choose to take a quick weekend trip with the girls or fly cross-country for that dream family vacation to Disney World. Certainly, some of us will embark on life-changing trips that allow us to see the world through a different, more expansive, or more sobering lens. But what if we choose to be formed first in the daily places and spaces we occupy? What if *where we are now* already points us to where our voices are needed most, the spaces most likely to receive us, where our impact over time saturates the ground of relationship versus simply staying on the surface of a keyboard or phone screen?

Few people on Facebook know your beautician or barber like you do. Insignificant numbers of people on Instagram know your partner and kids like you do. No one knows the vantage point you have from your desk or cubicle or ergo chair. You see what's happening in your neighborhood from the couch in your living room or your favorite seat at the local coffee shop. What if your workshop or office or wine club are places where you can continue in the long soul work shaping you but also where you can see that soul work shape the spaces around you?

People who understand the importance of place are integral to communal flourishing. We can learn a lot from John Perkins, a pioneer in the field of Christian community development who has been doing work akin to Benedict's stability vow for over forty years. Perkins's life work takes seriously the call of the prophet Jeremiah for God's people to "seek the peace and prosperity of the city to which I have carried you into exile . . . because if it prospers, you too will prosper."[8]

In what's known as the "theology of place,"[9] Perkins and those working within the Christian Community Development Association (CCDA) hold to eight components, the first of which is relocation. The idea of relocation includes people who have moved to a new community (relocators), have moved back to a community where they formerly lived (returners), or who stayed in the community they are from (remainers).

> [In relocation], the person lives—and becomes part of—the community he or she hopes to see transformed . . . [which] entails desiring for our neighbors and our neighbors' families what we desire for ourselves and our own families.[10]

Embedded in this idea is *staying*. Perkins and CCDA leadership encourage people to commit to their "monastery" for at least fifteen years—profoundly countercultural in a world as transient, technologically driven, and distracted as ours.

What would happen if everyone took a vow to intentionally and consistently influence physical spaces and real people where they already are? To show up at our own neighborhood association meetings or town hall gatherings to listen to the cares and concerns of those who call our blocks or our cities "home"? These spaces usually hold regular agenda topics that roll over from month to month, but different people often attend, giving a chance for strangers to take one step toward becoming familiar faces. Or what if we engaged online neighborhood or workplace groups that help people connect around events and key milestones? From participating in block parties to going to parades to choosing to take meetings at a local neighborhood coffee shop instead of at the office, we must be physically present in the spaces around us in order to become purposefully influential.

The Power of Proximity

Years after my time in Rwanda, I'm sitting in a different room. Instead of murderers or genocide victims, men and women from two sides of a different historical tension sit around a modestly sized boardroom table: a teacher, a nonprofit leader, a nurse, a daycare provider, a businessman, a musician, and others. The tension has existed for years, mostly silently, between two neighborhoods in our city: one populated with mostly upper-middle class white families; the other, with a healthy representation of lower-middle class families. The latter neighborhood is home to vastly more Black families and boasts of a generations-old park that's home to our favorite city pool. The other neighborhood *also* has its own park, merely one block south and three blocks east, but this one belongs to a well-funded private Christian school.

A Black neighbor at the table tells those gathered that she tells people on the streets, down on their luck for one reason or another, not to walk "that way" (*that* way being toward the upper-middle class neighborhood), as someone is sure to call the police on them. (A few weeks later, a white neighbor would admit to me that the upper-middle class neighborhood's relationship to those living just across the line has been dominated by fear.)

For years, white and Black neighbors-by-proximity hadn't quite considered each other neighbors at all. You'd be hard-pressed to find someone crossing Giddings Avenue with a casserole—in either direction.

But we are here, neighbors from either side, because we know what the tremors of divisiveness can create. We know our history: of redlining in the city and the subsequent socioeconomic implications—white families fleeing to the newly developed suburbs, leaving the Black families who stayed to pick up the economic slack. And we want better than what we were handed, not just seeing each other, not just recognizing the tensions among us and our mutual humanity but encouraging and celebrating each other. We want to weep together over the influx in gun violence, not hide. We want to rejoice at neighborhood block parties and clean-ups, not isolate. Racially, socioeconomically, generationally, we're different—but we don't want our differences to divide us.

That narrative of division is true nationally, globally. And we also know it's true in our neighborhoods right now. We don't yet know how we're going to overcome it; we just know that we're all here because we want to be. Because showing up, together, holding place and space over store-bought sugar cookies and cups of water is one of the first and hardest steps. Deo Gashagaza's words from 2017 are true for us, too:

> We still have a lot of things to do for our communities, for social cohesion. It's painful, but it's a journey of healing.

Proximity means we choose physical space and real people. We aren't ignoring the rest of the world's pain, but we're choosing to focus on where we can make the most difference—to go deep in the world right outside our windows.

We don't have to go far. We just start here.

Testing the Pillar: Place + Space

1. When you consider what's happening around the world, what areas or issues draw you closer? How might you advocate for those issues more intentionally from or within your context?

2. What are the spaces you frequent, that might make up your "monastery"? In what ways can you see these spaces functioning as a "workshop for the soul"?

3. How do you react to Benedict's vow of stability? What would that kind of vow look like in your context? What barriers (self-imposed or otherwise) might keep you from living out that kind of vow?

4. Jeremiah 29:7 encourages its listeners to "seek the peace and prosperity of the city . . . because if it prospers, you too will prosper" (NIV). What would it look like for your community to flourish? How can you see your flourishing tied to your community flourishing? In what ways is that interdependence not yet realized?

5. How might you wield the influence of your voice differently, from right where you are? What would it take to resist the overwhelming global need and see your own contexts as enough?

CHAPTER 10

VERIFIED

[on authenticity]

The messages keep coming:

9:00 A.M.

Hi!! I just wondered if you know that there's another profile with your name . . . ? It requested to follow me.

10:36 A.M.

Hi, Ashlee! You may have had others report this to you, but there's an account that's impersonating you.

8:51 P.M.

Hey Ashlee! Thought you should know there is someone who has copied your account. They just started following me—but then realized it wasn't you!

This isn't the first time. Over the last few months, there have been numerous fake accounts created with some variation of my social media handle. One got really fancy and tried to put only one "e" at the end of my first name. Whoever is behind these accounts put some thought into pretending to be me: They copied my profile photos and pictures from my feed so they could populate a new feed with the exact same pictures.

And people believe them. A couple of these accounts have thousands of followers. But inevitably, someone who knows me personally or is familiar enough with my online content notices the discrepancies.

You can imitate someone superficially, but it's hard to imitate their voice.

In the literary world, *voice* refers to "the rhetorical mixture of vocabulary, tone, point of view, and syntax that makes phrases, sentences, and paragraphs flow in a particular manner."[1] It's the way we "read" a certain author in our head, like Langston Hughes, Charles Dickens, Maya Angelou, or Bell Hooks. Different voices could say or write the same content but deliver it differently. The difference in delivery—the voice—changes how we receive the message.

Those who know me and my voice know something is off with these fake accounts, and I'm grateful they're reaching out to alert me. From what I can tell, the biggest tip-offs are always the messages people receive from "me," sometimes asking for money. Messages like:

Hello Beloved the Holy Spirit led me through your profile
I don't know you in person but God does.
The lord has a word for you,
there will be a divine breakthrough in your life this period,
keep trusting the Lord he never fails.
May the doors of favour open in your life in Jesus name, Amen.

From what you know of my voice so far, would you consider this message to be consistent? I sure hope not! I'm no captain of the grammar police, but those run-on sentences! The missing capitalization! The cheesy Christian "pickup" line! For a complete stranger, the message may seem legitimate enough, but for the most part? A fraud.

As each person alerts me to fake accounts and accompanying messages, I ask the same thing in hopes that, eventually, the account will be taken down, sparing unassuming Insta scrollers from its trap and bad grammar: "If you have time, please report them."

Our distinct voice matters. It's not enough to simply have a stance, opinion, encouragement, or perspective. Whether you're leading a team or leveraging your influence in your own family, sitting around a happy hour table with friends or engaging online with a mix of critics and comrades—your voice should sound like yours.

No impostors allowed.

Needed and Wanted

Imagine there's this creative kids cartoon on PBS, complete with talking limbs made of felt puppet material. First up, we meet Foot. Foot is made of important bones, muscles, and ligaments. And Foot connects the body to the ground, allowing the body to walk a golf course, run from a Super Soaker, or hold a yoga pose. But one day, Foot starts to go through an identity crisis. Even though Foot can move the body anywhere, it finds itself gazing enviously at Hand. *Hand can strum a guitar*, Foot thinks. *Hand can pick flowers, write love notes, paint murals.* Foot thinks Hand gets to do the body's most fun and essential tasks.

But Foot isn't the only one getting mixed up. There seems to be a similar situation happening with Ear. Ear gets to hear a new song for the first time at your favorite band's concert, a newborn's very first cry, the roar of a crowd at the NBA Finals. But Ear wants to see like Eye does: a stunning sunset over the Pacific Ocean; the first buds of spring bursting through melting snow; fireworks in a warm summer sky.

Our felt-puppet show would be chaos, wouldn't it?

The apostle Paul talks about this very thing in a letter he wrote to the church in Corinth, using the metaphor of a body and its parts to expound upon how each individual relates to the whole, and how that whole relates to Jesus Christ:

> If the foot says, "Because I am not a hand, I am not a part of the body," it is not for this reason any less a part of the body. And if the ear says, "Because I am not an eye, I am not a part of the body," it is not for this reason any less a part of the body. If the whole body were an eye, where would the hearing be? If the whole body were hearing, where would the sense of smell be?[2]

Here's what Paul is trying to get across: Each part is indispensable, even if it doesn't *think* it is.

Let's say, in our PBS show, that Foot could become Hand, and Ear gets her wish and becomes Eye for a day. Paul is trying to convey that, if that happened, the body would no longer work harmoniously. Even if a vital function weren't compromised, the parts need one another in order to affirm the vital function of parts that may be considered insignificant by those outside the body's system. Without that interconnectedness, we miss out on bearing witness to a reality that points us to the joy of the body's functioning as God designed.

Each part of the body isn't just needed; it's wanted.

Even if we don't know *exactly* why it exists (like an appendix), even if it seems like a last-minute add-on (hello, pinky toe)—every part of the body is good and valuable.

The way the body was made to work, the way we were made to relate to one another, isn't as individual pieces simply moving in and out of one another's spaces. We were meant to connect to each other's joints, meant to be tied through tissues and nurtured through veins. And that kind of mysterious, purposeful connection can only be realized if you live out of the part designed uniquely, specifically, particularly just for you.

Because if you tried to be anything else, we wouldn't run, we wouldn't hear, we would miss vision and inspiration and insight. The body just wouldn't be the same without you.

Scared to Be Seen

In 2015, a British woman named Jules O'Dwyer won both the country's hearts and votes by wowing spectators with the talents of a very special guest. Jules and her beloved brown-and-white border collie Matisse were on the fast track to stardom, just one performance away from clenching the title as winners of *Britain's Got Talent* season nine. With freestyle tricks and masterful storytelling, Jules and Matisse sailed through their audition round and then two semifinal rounds to secure a spot in the highly anticipated finale.

For the final episode, Jules played a policewoman and Matisse played the role of a four-legged runaway sausage thief. After a few moments, the act came to a gasp-inducing climax. As over thirteen million viewers watched, Matisse walked his way across two parallel tightropes onstage.

The feat was enough to capture both the win and £250,000 in cash, though the voting margins were close. Jules and Matisse won by only 2 percent, making the victory even more meaningful.

All seemed celebratory until just days later—when it was revealed that Matisse was not, in fact, the tightrope-walking canine. Since Matisse was reportedly afraid of heights, Jules had instead tagged in Matisse's look-alike and stunt double, Chase, to complete the tightrope walking portion of the scene.

The public's response in the wake of the news of the switcheroo was swift and serious: Ofcom (the United Kingdom's Office of Communications) received over a thousand complaints from disgruntled fans accusing Jules of misleading them since they had cast votes for Matisse.[3]

Though Jules received support from judges and was still deemed the winner of the season, some found the exchange hard to forgive. When heartstrings are attached and expectations are set, even the most impressive takes need the real deal. Perhaps the crux of the issue isn't about social media or dogs. Perhaps those infractions point to yet another reminder of just how vital our *distinct* function is to the overall design.

A lot of us find it difficult to own that distinct part we have to offer. We struggle to identify—let alone speak—from the joy and security of core self.

We're so used to seeing substitutes advertised and marketed as ideal—from glamorized false lashes that tell us our own lashes aren't long enough to hair implants for balding men that remind them of their mop of yesteryear—we start to think our core self isn't enough, that a substitute or upgrade is needed.

Psychologists call this special brand of self-doubt "impostor syndrome." Psychologist Pauline Clance originally coined this idea as "impostor phenomenon." Along with her colleague Suzanne Imes, Clance spent five years researching and recording stories of more than 150 women who'd experienced a certain level of success in fields like law, social work, and nursing. But that research revealed something curious. According to Clance and Imes, the women interviewed all had "'an internal experience of intellectual phoniness,' living in perpetual fear that 'some significant person will discover that they are indeed intellectual impostors.'"[4] Although their research targeted only women, they identified a larger pattern: Impostor syndrome produces "a sense of impending failure that inspires frenzied hard work, and short-lived gratification when failure is staved off, quickly followed by the return of the old conviction that failure is imminent."[5]

Since Clance and Imes, more recent voices have thoughtfully critiqued the idea of impostor syndrome (for example, identifying the influence of systemic factors versus individual self-doubt).[6] But regardless, naming these signs draws our focus to an important reality: that beneath our layers of hustle and hard work, our degrees and our death grip on the guise of success, we are often really scared.

We can be scared even when there's zero reason to be. What if someone were to shine a bright light on all the ways we've failed? What if we're never as good as we or someone else thinks we should be? Or worse, what if we were good that one time and are never that good at anything ever again?

So you're scared your social media post won't read the right way? You care about community flourishing or acts of justice and mercy, but you're scared your privilege will disqualify you? You're convinced your words will be taken out of context, that where you are on your learning journey isn't quite far enough for other people to journey with you?

You're a dang good foot, but you're pretty sure you haven't run fast enough. And what if someone looked at those toes and saw how badly you needed a pedicure?

You know people want Matisse to walk the tightrope . . . and you aren't Matisse.

And so you type . . . and delete.

You call . . . and hang up.

You stay silent, you minimize.

You wish you were a hand.

What's Real and True

When we're too scared to live and talk from our authentic self, we risk everyone else missing out on a perspective that helps all of us see God's work in the world more fully. We risk losing our connectedness, how what you have to offer brings new depth to what I have to offer.

But there's another risk in this pursuit of authenticity: that we overcompensate for our self-doubt and fear by pretending it doesn't exist. When that happens, humility has a way of flying straight out the window. We leave self-examination behind as we speed along in the semitruck of our ego.

When this happens, what we're left with are voices that speak without care and concern for the truth—or for other people. Voices that refuse to listen to or learn from anyone else. Voices that care more about being impressive than having integrity. Voices that are simply content to join the larger chorus of hashtags or crowd chants or network news anchors.

Authenticity isn't just about saying what you *really* feel.

Authenticity is about discerning the intersection of what's real and true, both in what we're speaking into (contexts, situations, relationships), and in what we're speaking out of (our motivations, wounds, passions).

But I'd even take it one step further. Because—remember Paul now—no part of the body was designed to serve itself but each was made to participate in the flourishing of the whole. Speaking and living authentically isn't ultimately about serving ourselves.

We don't lean into authenticity to get something off our chest.

We don't lean into authenticity for short-lived gratification such as likes or reposts or comments.

We lean into authenticity to participate in the flourishing of the whole—to bring the body back in line with what it was intended to do.

Authenticity is about discerning the intersection of what's real and true, both in what we're speaking into and in what we're speaking out of, *for the health and wholeness of the entire body.*

Consider what would happen if the heart withheld blood from the rest of the body, if it were tempted to—for whatever reason—keep all the blood for itself. This would endanger not just the heart, but the rest of the body. Only the heart offering what it's meant to offer allows the body to function as it should. In the same way, generous and wise authenticity allows us to disperse to the rest of body what we can give (our skill, perspective, resources), which helps us thrive as we're meant to in community while also sharing something vital that the rest of the community needs. Do you believe that the function you play is vital to the health of the whole body?

Similarly, say our eyes refused to blink in sync with each other because they wanted to be distinct. Function wouldn't necessarily be impacted, but the design would be altered. There are ways we are meant to work together, to put on display the beautiful function of the body and our interconnectedness. If we find that we are spending most of our time by ourselves, neither inviting others into partnership nor saying yes to *any* invitations for partnership, we may be missing out on the opportunity to live into wholeness together.

On some social media platforms, there's a process called verification—something that tells the average person scrolling, *This person is who they say they are.* And (I know this now after the battles against all those fake accounts) verification is *difficult.* After a person submits legitimate identification—and blocks, reports, and exposes fake accounts—verification confirms that this account is a real, true presence occupied by a real, true person. Verification is really for the health and wholeness of the entire community.

So how do we discern the intersection of what's true and what's real, both in what we're speaking into and in what we're speaking out of—and do so in a way that serves the health and wholeness of our community for good?

Even given our modern-day struggles with identifying and speaking truth, we all have the capacity to, somehow, some way, grow in noticing what we're speaking out of—what's really and truly happening within ourselves. Speaking even good things in too many places can leave an eager spirit tired and parched. Are we allowing anyone to say good to (or into) us? Whether through mentors or other willing teachers, friends, or family members ahead of us in years and wisdom, what is being spoken into us contributes to our wholeness—and the wholeness of the entire body in the long run. For me, this has looked like choosing to be in therapy with some regularity over the past thirteen years, inviting a trained professional to help me process patterns and pains, and learn better strategies to care for my own mental and emotional health. (I'm grateful that we, particularly in the church, are doing better at destigmatizing conversations around hard topics like mental health, depression, anxiety, and suicide.) I've also invited spiritual directors to help hold certain parts of my journey with me.

They encourage me to engage the discipline of listening just as much as (if not more than) I speak.

In a similar way, we can take stock of what we're speaking into, looking outside ourselves to the health and wholeness of the entire community: other peoples' lives, community endeavors, work projects, ideas to raise awareness for causes we care about and injustices we feel must be addressed. Who are those in our immediate midst who are deprived of basic needs, access, and opportunity? What's being hoarded—and by whom? Where are we able to see a generous flow of mutuality: from heart to bones, from brain to limbs? Healthy, whole communities find ways to find, include, celebrate, and learn from *everyone*. Those in need of healing are provided aid through acts of hospitality like companionship, the provision of resources, and opportunities to find beauty and play. Those who are vulnerable are made to feel safe and secure. The weak are strengthened by the whole, enveloped and not forgotten. Each community will do this differently—but all can look healthy and whole in their own unique contexts.

But *how* we move forward into all this requires not just discernment but some points of practical wisdom, too. If, for example, you've never talked publicly or freely about racial injustice of your own initiative, you may not wish to first enter the conversation on the public square of social media, with open access to complete strangers. You probably want to avoid presenting an opinion as a supposed expert if what you *really* sense is that you need to learn more in real life with real people. Some "verification" filters can help us as we learn where our authentic voice should take up space:

- The **"when no one's watching" filter.** Ask yourself how many times you've lamented or ranted or raged or cried without packaging those reactions up for public consumption. If you more often turn to social media or other more impersonal outlets, consider taking a season where you keep your reactions close and process them with trusted companions.

- **The motives filter.** Interrogate the true motives behind what and how you share, whatever form that takes. A good test for online interaction is to leave the conversation, post, or tweet in Drafts for a day. If, after honest self-examination, you realize that the communication was actually for "likes" or engagement—that you'd move quickly past how that offering makes the community you're reaching more whole—you may want to sit on it until you can engage the entire body, not just your part.

- **The in-person filter.** How willing would you be to have a conversation with someone else *in person* with the very words you plan to write or type or text? If the way you're imagining engaging is already in-person, is what you're longing to express connected to a real desire for that person's good? If you notice your internal narrative centers around longing for an opportunity to prove yourself, or even if you can't name a clear motive at all, consider what would need to be tended to internally before an in-person conversation could be healthy, mutually loving, and productive. If you would say something online but not in an in-person conversation, ask yourself, "Why?" Are you unwilling to be challenged? Would you not have much to talk about because you don't actually know them well enough?

- **The process filter.** Consider how raw a certain topic feels for you. Particularly if there is fresh or unprocessed pain or trauma, what of your own healing needs to first take place before you lead the way for others? If the timing feels too soon, if you feel anxiety about others' responses (or lack thereof); if you discern using your voice would be only a cathartic outlet for you to process pain when it may be best processed with trusted others, resist any collective calls to urgency and take the time and space you need to start (or continue) healing.

As you learn to fine-tune the unique part your voice plays in this world, your voice—practiced over time and in arenas both seen and unseen—should sound like yours. To those who trust you enough to listen, your voice should sound comfortingly familiar and not jarringly forced, even if the message itself is hard or tender. As you pay attention to your voice, ask, "Is this the spirit with which I want to lead? Are these the unseen yet felt sound waves I want people to hear from the reverberations of my presence? Did I offer what I was longing to say from a healing—even if not fully healed—place?"

If we choose to influence the world around us with the familiar tones of authenticity, we'll keep away impostors . . . and we'll remember that the impostor was never us to begin with.

Testing the Pillar: Authenticity

1. What words would you use to characterize your unique voice as you speak and write into different contexts? Is your voice poetic? Punchy? Academic? Thoughtful? Think about images, textures, sounds, and scenes that might accompany your voice. If you get stuck in this exercise, think about how you'd ideally like your voice to sound. (For example: *I'd like my voice to mimic water flowing in a river: comforting and*

accessible at certain points, dynamic and full at others, but always inviting and nourishing.)

2. Reflect on any situations in which you felt like an impostor. How did you act or relate differently in those situations? What did it take for you to work through the self-doubt? Write down the people, practices, or words of truth that helped you then. Mark them for the future when you might need them again.

3. Imagine a body. What part of that body are you? (As a deep feeler, writer, communicator, and mother, I often imagine myself as hands, assisting in all those roles.) Is there a part you regularly wish you could be instead? Imagine the body part you identify with most strongly and work with this prompt in whatever way is most helpful:

   As a _____, I serve the body best when I _____.

4. Which of the four filters resonates most with you? How can you begin putting the filter into practice today?

CHAPTER 11

PANDEMIC PUPPY AND PAUL (AGAIN)

[on power dynamics]

Back in the early pandemic days of 2020, everyone had their own brand of quarantining. For our family of five, our experience looked like a lot of other peoples': navigating working at home while also attempting to keep three kids entertained and healthily stimulated.

As creatives, my husband and I spent a lot of time locking ourselves in the basement, the living room, the bedroom, even the bathroom— ideally within that perfect window of time when our kids were either outside in the yard playing or inside napping—so we could press that familiar red button and record a song, a sermon, a conference talk. Ring lights traveled up and down the stairs with us, illuminating our front bay windows late into the night (maybe freaking out our neighbors). We were deliriously desperate, trying to make anything work: me in blouse and blazer on top and high school sweatpants and bare feet on bottom, trying to appear professional and adequately present during online conference presentations, Zoom meetings with staff, and FaceTime with family. There was at least one moment when I was lying on my couch, laptop on my thighs as I attempted to write a sermon while a small child *sat on my chest*. I just kept typing because I couldn't escape. (I'd like to reemphasize the word *desperate* here.)

I baked or made dessert from scratch almost every day as a coping mechanism.

I'm embarrassed to admit we watched *Tiger King* to take the edge off.

We bought random, frivolous things for our home just to "switch it up, honey; I think we need something to bond over together as a family." That's how we procured a snow cone machine, a camping tent for our living room (yes, for the *inside* of our house, folks), and a whole climbing dome for our back yard.

We didn't bake sourdough.

By the end of that year, I'd made another decision that would change the course of our lives forever. As someone who'd been managing anxiety and depression since high school, I knew I'd need a strategy that would get me out of the house as the warm winds of summer transitioned to fall rains, chills, and changing leaves, to eventually winter's freezing temperatures and inches of snow.

I needed a reason to get out and walk our neighborhood, no matter how cold it was.

I needed a companion that would listen and not protest, one I didn't need to hide from in a locked bathroom just so I could think and eat my Girl Scout cookies.

I needed . . . a pandemic puppy.

My husband and parents tried to talk me out of it, but I would not be deterred. And so my husband cast his only wish: "It needs to be big dog."

I researched and studied and asked around and polled neighbors. We needed a hypoallergenic breed for the family members with allergies. We needed a breed with a fun-loving personality that was good with small kids.

We went on a waitlist for a Bernedoodle (a Bernese mountain dog–poodle mix). Our breeder told us the puppies would come around Christmas. Perfect. We'd surprise the kids, and it would be the best Christmas ever.

And in some ways, it was. Our puppy came home to us as eight pounds of black, brown, and tan fluff. We dubbed him Chance the Rap-paw in honor of Chicago rapper Chance the Rapper, because my husband *also* requested his name pay homage to his hometown, Chicago. (Phil Jackson was a close second, but what would we sound like yelling, "Phil!" across the park?!)

Chance was beloved from the beginning . . . by *almost* everybody.

You see, there's another dog in the family: a thirteen-year-old, technically overweight Yorkie-poo (Yorkshire terrier–poodle mix) that I brought home when I first moved to Chicagoland as a single woman. Jasper is what we call the OG, the "original gangster," the much-loved first dog of my adulthood. Jasper and I had been through a lot of life together, all the way up until Delwin and I had our first daughter. That's when my parents graciously offered to take Jasper back to Texas with them "just for a little while," while we got used to being a family of three.

That little while turned into eight years. My family loves dogs, and Jasper, quite frankly, hated the snow.

When Jasper accompanied my parents for Christmas that year, Chance was an immediate interloper. Jasper was first, he was older, and we were *his* family. What was more, Chance was not a small puppy. He was already almost bigger than Jasper from day one. As the months progressed, Jasper grew chubbier in his old age, and Chance grew taller.

To voice his disapproval, Jasper would nip at Chance's legs or sit in front of him, blocking Chance from getting to anyone in the family. Conversely, he'd put his paws on my legs and insist I pick him up so he could snuggle in close and stare at Chance in defiance. He'd uncharacteristically urinate in the kitchen—once even on the living-room rug—in protest.

Eventually, at around eighty pounds, Chance stopped growing. His long poodle legs towered above Jasper's pudgy frame. If Chance even accidentally backed into him, Jasper would get frustrated. Chance's human-palm-sized paws were more than large enough to trip up the old curmudgeon.

Even though Jasper was older and had had more time and memories with our family, sometimes sheer size and strength won out in the struggle for power and dominance. Without trying, the new canine on the block demanded presence and respect, for no other reason than he was huge. Commanding. Powerful without even trying.

On one hand, his presence accomplished exactly what I'd hoped. He'd rest his head or his paws on my lap, and the weight of him would ground me, reminding me to be present in my body. I felt safe on our walks outside in the snow, could be by myself with just my mess of thoughts and heavy-heartedness.

But on the other hand, Chance's power—at least for one smaller, more vulnerable creature—wasn't comforting at all. His power was a threat, a source of fear, too overwhelming to be welcomed closer.

To this day, I still watch as power plays in ways the two dogs may not realize: one unknowingly wielding power he didn't earn; another anxious, assessing threat.

Power dynamics are shifting and seismic, often unnoticed and unnamed. Some people bring power to situations without recognizing it, without even trying, whether through position, background, presence, or some other weight of authority. On the other hand, some people notice the anxiety of that weight, acting in fearful or uncertain ways but not always understanding that it's a perception of power they're reacting to. All that people see, from both perspectives, is that relationships fracture, tension builds, and things fall apart. All because power is lurking there, causing chaos from under the surface.

The Power of Power

Power, wielded well, can be lifesaving. Nik Wallenda and his team knew that his walks at the Grand Canyon would require more than just a man and a rope. Engineering and expertise and an undergirding power would be needed to set him up for success.

One part of the Grand Canyon that Wallenda needed to cross was completely inaccessible by road. Wallenda would begin his walk in an area of the Canyon called Hell Hole Bend, a mesa surrounded by nothing but cliffs. How could his team possibly secure the wire cable in those conditions?

That's when electricians entered the picture. I know what you're thinking: electricians? On a death-defying high-wire project?

Because trucks couldn't access the mesa, the team had to use helicopters and find these specialists—not your everyday lightbulb installers, mind you—who could creatively troubleshoot a solution. What came next was an intricate process that only certain electricians, people literally in charge of handling power, could pull off:

> On both sides of the gorge, 6-foot tall wooden paddle block
> pyramids were constructed to provide clearance from the
> ground and the edge of the cliff. Anchors, placed into the
> earth and reinforced by concrete, were also installed on both

sides. Workers suspended in baskets from the cable installed counterbalance bars across the span.[1]

Power literally grounded and secured the very stage upon which bravery and skill would be on display. When power is stewarded intentionally, it can provide stability and safety in the midst of risk.

But power used recklessly, unaware of or uncaring about its impact, creates the opposite effect: putting voices, people, communities in great danger.

Defined simply, *power* is the level of control one person has over another person.[2] While we could certainly throw more bells and whistles into the mix, power, stripped all the way down, is about control in relationships. But not all power comes from the same source. In 1959, social psychologists John French and Bertram Raven identified five bases of power:

1. Coercive (relying on force)
2. Reward (relying on incentives)
3. Legitimate (relying on hierarchy)
4. Referent (relying on one's affiliation)
5. Expert (relying on authority)

Years later, French and Raven added a sixth source of power:

6. Informational (relying on access to scarce resources of data)[3]

This list can give us a starting point for assessing what kind of power we hold or interact with in our contexts. We must also keep in mind specific types of social power (political, socioeconomic, gender-based, racial, etc.) that create even more opportunities for us to evaluate our stories, backgrounds, and ways social status plays into our possibility for influence. As the Urban Institute notes,

> Power plays a significant role in how and by whom policy decisions are made. In part, inequities exist because of the power imbalance in public decisionmaking.[4]

Our country has built-in power inequities due to our history: generations where some held (and still hold) significant power, building it exponentially over time, through strategic business moves or simply through inheritance—while others were intentionally and systemically erased or pushed to the margins. Unfortunately, because these inequities were both built in and passed down, those who've historically held the most power struggle to understand or even be aware of that reality, which leads to minimizing and even delegitimizing important considerations around power and historically excluded voices.

You are reading this book because you want to be part of good, positive change. What that means, though, is that some of us have to sit with the ways—even unexamined—that we operate from a place of power. Only then can we steward our power on purpose, *with* purpose, noticing when it helps and when it hurts, wielding it or laying it down appropriately.

I implore you: Do the work to explore the power you have either inherited, been handed, or earned. That kind of self-awareness is crucial to walking effectively into tensions and complexities. In the work of saying good, it's a piece that needs to be acknowledged and said. Even if you're not the CEO of your organization (legitimate power), you may work in a department that is the holder of sensitive information (informational). If you currently don't or choose not to have a job, you may still hold a level of referent power—whether because of the social circles you run in; the school you graduated from and its associated alumni connections; the neighborhood you live in and what that says about your likely (or unlikely) affiliations with wealth; your access to goods and services, like healthcare; or the kind of physical security you have.

As we determine how to engage with our areas of influence, we must humbly and thoroughly consider what power dynamics we introduce into those places. This is no one else's job but our own. Stewarding our voices requires awareness of when our strength might make another person flinch.

Conversations about power can get really tense, really quickly. Just peek at this country's last one hundred years of protest movements about grave and significant gaps in access or ability to exercise basic human rights. Make power personal, and it's easy to rock back in defense: "But I wasn't directly responsible for the oppression of an entire people!" "I worked hard to earn what I have!" "I've struggled too!" And any of these objections may be 100 percent true. But here's what understanding power means: It's possible not to be directly responsible and still benefit from something. Power gained through oppressive means doesn't just disappear with the oppression. For example, slave owners accumulated exponential wealth and social power over centuries, and that power paid literal dividends even after slavery officially became illegal in the United States in 1865. That wealth, that social power, benefited their descendants, whether those descendants realized it or not. In America, many have subscribed to the "American way" of considering themselves self-made, even though we all hold what generations before us have passed down: whether that be a trust fund or trauma or—in some cases—both.

Even those of us with power in some spaces can still be disempowered in other ways. As a Black woman in America whose descendants were brutally captured and brought over to America to carry out forced labor, I don't have access to generations worth of my family history. I don't have the privilege of knowing my original African "name," because my ancestors were given the names of their owners and masters. Family legacy and history and names—as we see with the likes of Carnegie, Roosevelt, Kennedy, and Ford—hold a unique power, a memory, a weight of influence.

Taking a Look at Power

Remember how the apostle Paul talks about all the parts of the body as necessary and indispensable? He keeps going, and what he says ends up helping us discern more about the power we bring with our voice:

> I also want you to think about how [understanding the interdependence of the parts of the body] keeps your significance from getting blown up into self-importance. For no matter how significant you are, it is only because of what you are a *part* of. . . . No part is important on its own. . . . As a matter of fact, in practice it works the other way—the "lower" the part, the more basic, and therefore necessary. . . . When it's a part of your own body you are concerned with, it makes *no* difference whether the part is visible or clothed, higher or lower. You give it dignity and honor just as it is, without comparisons. If anything, you have more concern for the lower parts than the higher. If you had to choose, wouldn't you prefer good digestion to full-bodied hair?[5]

I don't actually know if I could answer Paul's last question the way he hoped—but sure, I guess good digestion is ultimately more important than a fabulous mane of crochet braids. But here's what he means: Our individual power isn't the point. We must remember what we're part of. What's more, at least when it comes to becoming like Jesus in how we move through this world, it's the lesser parts—the parts that may seem to hold less power—that might actually deserve more of our concern.

Consider the pineal gland, which is the smallest organ in the body. That gland is in the center of your brain and functions as the main control center for the secretion of melatonin, which controls your body's internal clock and helps you fall asleep at night. Small organ. Powerful impact.

When we choose how and when to speak—to, for, and on behalf of others—we need to pay attention to how our part affects the whole. That means we have to be intentional about examining the power we hold in those relationships. Psychologists often identify three types of power dynamics that hold the potential to cause strained or dangerously imbalanced relationships:

- The **demand-withdrawal** dynamic, where one person is persistent in pursing change or resolution. In contrast, the other person is usually withdrawn or avoidant.

- The **distancer-pursuer** dynamic, where one person pursues a level of intimacy or closeness that the other person finds unwelcome or overbearing. (Extreme cases of this type may lead to harassment or abuse.)

- The **fear-shame** dynamic, where one person exploits the fears or sources of shame of the other person. (This can lead to withdrawal or aggression.)[6]

Although these dynamics typically show up in intimate relationships, we can also consider their broader application as we use our voices. Someone ranting on Facebook or Instagram to no one in particular is exercising both demand-withdrawal and distance-pursuer power dynamics. Someone using people's fears to motivate them toward a potentially destructive response is operating out of a fear-shame power dynamic.

If we refuse to evaluate and acknowledge the power we hold, we should be sparse with the words we choose to say. Our words are the wings upon which power flies, influencing the formation of communities or the destruction of hearts. Wisdom and care for other human beings should caution us from speaking out of an unexamined place.

Power for Good

We've been focusing a lot on the ways power can go wrong, but I want to draw us back to how, when we pay attention to power dynamics and the power we operate out of, power can be a force for good.

At the first church that ever employed me, one of my mentors told me that I had the spiritual gift of teaching. But I didn't quite understand what to do with that gift, how exactly to use it. I hadn't gone to seminary at that point; I didn't know how to craft a sermon, let alone a good one; and I had hardly seen *any* examples of women leading in the church.

Enter a white guy named Steve. When Steve was hired to teach at the church full-time, people were excited about his arrival. Steve was a brilliant communicator, dynamic in his delivery, masterful at telling stories. In his role, he held legitimate power—both on the org chart and even in his physical office location. His office was on the well-lit, window-laden third floor. I, in contrast, was hammering it out in the basement, under a literal single flickering fluorescent light.

And then, one day, Steve came down to the basement.

Under that single flickering fluorescent light, he took an Expo marker that was on its last legs and taught me about teaching. He drew two diagrams (one about the emotional arcs of a good story; one relating to persuasive versus enabling content structure) that I still use to this day.

He was important. People loved him. In our church and in our dynamic, he had power. And there he was, giving me his best stuff, on his own time, for free.

A couple of years later, after I'd cut my teeth teaching a few times in our community, Steve asked me if I wanted to tag-teach with him at a high-school conference in Indiana. I was so darn scared. There were eleven sessions total, and the conference was taking place at a camp near and dear to his heart.

"I'll split it with you," I said. I could do five sessions if he'd agree to do six.

"Deal," he said. Arrangements were made. We were set to speak together that summer.

But then—and I still to this day wonder if this was a legitimate conflict or if it was more strategic on his part—"something came up." I'd be teaching the camp alone. Take *scared* and raise it to *beyond terrified*. But, calmly, over the phone, he told me I could do it.

This white man took his power-turned-privilege and, for whatever reason, chose to hand me an opportunity I would not have secured otherwise. He took something from a position of advantage and influence and offered it to scruffy, inexperienced little me. He did it because he believed in me as a woman—a Black woman—in ministry.

Steve was a humble leader who knew how to use his power for good. And like those electricians over the Grand Canyon, he helped ready me for both the very stage upon which I'd walk and talk that summer—and further into my vocation.

Power can be an electrifying, holy, and beautiful thing. What matters is how we choose to see it—and how we choose to use it.

Testing the Pillar: Power Dynamics

1. Whether you're familiar with power dynamics or new to the concept, what is your gut reaction when asked to consider where you have power? Take some time and space to work through your reactions. Where do you think your reaction is coming from?

2. Consider French and Raven's six bases of power. Which ones can you identify as part of your personal influence? Which parts might have surprised you? As you consider categories of social power, what additional layers might be applied?

3. Thinking through Paul's perspective on the dignity and honor of lesser parts, how do his words translate to your own context? Is there anyone in your life or community who has a gift, skill, or function that would be considered a "lesser part" today? How does this perspective challenge you? Encourage you?

4. Where do you see the three types of power imbalances at work in your personal life or in our society in general? What might you imagine as remedies to these dynamics?

5. Do you have any "Steves" in your life? How have you witnessed someone using their power for your good or on your behalf?

6. Write one practical way you can use your power to make space for someone who has less power than you do in a certain area. If no one specific comes to mind, how can you consistently elevate someone you are learning from who has a historically excluded voice?

PART V

Relationship

Guard them as they pursue this life . . .
so they can be one heart and mind.
JOHN 17:11, MSG

The love of one person can heal. It heals the scars left
by a larger society. A massive, powerful society.
MAYA ANGELOU

The PAIR Pillars

Passion
Accountability
Influence
Relationship

General headlines encourage general responses and general thinking. If we engage our passions and our voices outside the context of real relationships, we'll be tempted to live in a space absent the very creation that God so loved: people.

Stewarding our voices should draw us back into the soil-smudged and yet fruit-bearing ecosystem of relationship, not further from it. As we spend our energy and take bold steps forward in an arena where we also invest deeply in relationships, we'll discover legacy-sized implications for our families and friends, our neighbors and communities.

Leaning on this final pillar means we resolve to listen more than we speak, to hold tension in one hand and a pack of tissues in the other, to allow our silence to say more than we ever could've imagined with our words. Jesus came for people, to create a path across what was once an inconceivable canyon: between a perfect God and fallen humanity. The cross bridged that canyon for the sake of the world. Now we join him in the work of bridging canyons—between people, across divides.

The steadying pillar of relationship equips us to defy the very black-and-white boundaries that have been drawn for us. We must locate our heartbeats, our best and truest selves, and our spaces of influence inside the messy, miraculous, and complex design of human relationships.

CHAPTER 12

NOT-SO-HAPPY HOUR

[on confession]

The rain is coming down hard on this mid-October day. Sheets of water slide down the front windshield like a mini Slip 'N Slide, but no one passing by on the sidewalk seems to be having any fun. The clouds are low and gray, typical for this time of year. I couldn't feel more helpless.

I've been scared of this happening. Anxiety and depression have been with me since college, and I know this form—as I've heard from many neighbors, friends, and even mere acquaintances—can show up under the weight of dreary days.[1]

Here in my car, I panic, anticipating many more days, weeks, and months of feeling not just low, but lost. And this moment feels similar to my past experiences with depression too—a sense of profound sadness mixed with a hyperawareness of how absurd it is to feel this profoundly sad. Self-judgment crams into the passenger seat next to me along with that sadness, just sitting there, waiting for me to do something—anything.

I can't will my way out.

I rest my head on the steering wheel and start bawling, letting the heaves work through my chest. "Why am I like this?" I choke out, to no one in particular but maybe to God.

Of all the reasons why this bout on this day is particularly inconvenient, my job would be at the top of the list. I'm a pastor of a church community.

I grew up in churches where the pastor had it together, was the most hopeful, well-dressed, and faith-filled person in the building. On top of that, the Black churches in which I was raised tended not to talk about anxiety, depression, or any accompanying suicidal ideation; somehow, to experience any of it meant you didn't have enough faith, didn't know how to take thoughts captive, didn't have what it took to be a good Christian.

Why am I like this?

As the sobs slow and my chest returns to its regular rise and fall, I notice that the rain does too.

At home, my husband listens compassionately as I tell him what happened in the car, both how these moments are simultaneously so intense and yet embarrassingly mundane. He knows my journey well, the ups and downs: the times my depression has gone into remission, giving me hope that maybe it'll be gone for good; the times it pops up and surprises me, an unwelcome confetti cannon of despair.

After listening well, he asks if I'm going to tell anyone else about this day. He's always ready and willing to sit with me in this. But in this moment, he's inviting me into a different risk with my voice, the kind that has nothing to do with an opinion, a cause, a holy discontent. He's inviting me to confess to other safe people so that the darkness won't keep me hidden, so I might experience the power of bringing something hard, tense, and risky into the light.

"Tell your friends," he encourages me.

I know which three friends he means. We've known each other for close to a decade, celebrating the arrival of babies, mourning the loss of babies; cheering the start of new jobs, encouraging at the leaving of old ones. We've walked each other through conflicts with our families, lived out memories and key moments as they unfolded.

I travel back to Chicago for one night to see them. The updates begin with lighthearted and exciting things. One of my friends is about to launch her first book into the world, and we are so proud of her. Another friend talks about hard stuff like navigating a family member's addiction—and good stuff, like updates on her boys and their impressive athletic pursuits. The third friend processes through motherhood challenges. Yet while she is talking, my heart begins pounding without prompting, a kick-drum making its way to my eardrums. I shove some chicken into my mouth so I have an excuse to break eye contact.

Why am I so nervous? What do I fear will happen? I realize I'm less scared of their reactions and more preemptively mourning having to relive the sadness and shame. I'm scared my confession will put a damper on a night when we have so little time. I try to force down the fear along with the food.

"Ash?"

I take a deep breath.

"I'm struggling," I begin. And then, in the moments and sentences that follow, I tell them everything.

One by one, they place their hands on my hand, my knee. Their tears roll down with mine. One of my friends pulls me close, resting my head on her shoulder. As I let the salt hit my lips, and my nose flows freely, making a mess that weighs down tissue after tissue, somehow I feel lighter than I ever have.

We decide on a word together, a promise I confess to keep when it comes to my life, my life in relationship with them.

I promise that I'll *stay*.

Sharing Burdens

> For when I kept silent, my bones wasted away
> through my groaning all day long.[2]

These words come from a beautiful book in the Bible, one made up of psalms, poetic songs, and writings detailing various people's experiences. Some of those experiences are cause for gladness and celebration, but others point to the harder human struggles.

In this particular psalm, a man named David writes of his wrongdoings—and how holding in the hard parts of his own failures have made an impact on his life. His words point to emotional turmoil, unrest, physical deterioration.

Here David indirectly encourages us to speak up—and not just because we have something to say or about what's happening *out there*. There are also places within us marked by distance: between who we want to be and who we are today; between us at our best and us on our worst days; between pain and healing, defeat and victory.

This kind of tightrope walking asks us to step forward gently, carefully, bravely across the divides in ourselves—and away from the idea that a single human being can make that walk alone, hidden, self-sufficient in how we posture and present ourselves to the watching world. David continues:

> I acknowledged my sin to you,
>> and I did not cover my iniquity;
> I said, "I will confess my transgressions to the LORD,"
>> and you forgave the iniquity of my sin.[3]

Instead of gritting his teeth and going through his pain alone, David chooses to pull out the darkest parts of him—not to display for faceless strangers, but in the context of a loving, intimate, and secure relationship. Here, that relationship is with God.

In this verse, David makes three intentional choices that we can apply not just to our own shortcomings and struggles—how we talk about them and who we choose to share them with—but also to all the other ways in which we choose to put our voices on the line. In the context of a loving, intimate, and secure relationship, David

- **chooses to acknowledge** (or "make known") **what's wrong;**
- **chooses not to hide;** and
- **chooses to confess** (or "throw, cast") **his struggles.**

David's actions give us a good framework for *where* and *how* we situate tough conversations. With God, we confess so that our life remains in the light of truth before the One who knows everything and loves us anyway. And though God is the one who forgives sin, we have been commissioned as followers of Christ to forgive one another, just as God, in Christ, forgave us.[4] Both confession and the giving and receiving of forgiveness strengthen our relationships with God and one another—building healthy and whole relationships between people and parts, further strengthening the body in its interconnectedness.

Acknowledge

First, David **acknowledges** (makes known) what's wrong to a particular person. We see here the importance of situating shortcomings in the context of actual relationship. What happens when we ignore this wisdom? Well, we've likely all witnessed someone revealing a personal struggle or dissatisfaction with sweeping statements in a general context (such as a post, tweet, revelatory announcement at the dinner table, or company-wide email directed at no one in particular . . . but you *definitely* know who they're talking about). Failing to locate topics and tension within the context of real relationship not only undermines the hope of real change taking place (within and between real people) but also robs us of the built-in accountability and support that might mutually form us in return.

Don't Hide

Next, David chooses **not to hide**. He didn't cover up what was wrong. Often we may be tempted to hide behind a screen, projecting only what we want someone to see through our words. I'm embarrassed to admit the number of times I've refused to share something hard (whether having been hurt by someone or being wrecked by another news headline), even with people I considered loving and secure. I tend to fake it till I make it, and in some ways, this has served me well. But if I ever decide to perpetually withhold what is on my heart, I know that—like David—I will waste away.

Confess

Finally, David chooses to **confess**—or literally "cast" his struggles—before God, sharing them outside himself. Again, we should be careful to never elevate imperfect humans to the level of deity—and we should be watchful for unhealthy codependence—but confessing the weights we're carrying *is* powerful, assuming the person we're sharing with is someone we trust and is willing to carry those burdens with us. How different this is from casting struggles far and wide, offering our words and opening our hearts to the potentially unfiltered commentary of complete strangers, to those who may not care for us or care for our wholeness!

Confession is powerful. Much later in the Bible, in the book of Galatians, the apostle Paul encourages the community there to "bear one another's burdens, and so fulfill the law of Christ."[5] We are invited into the same. These burdens we shoulder can be just plain heavy: pain, wounds, sickness, grief, and disappointment. Or they can be heavy but good, responsibilities entrusted to our care: our stories, our callings, our voices, the messages we've been asked or given to speak out for the good of those around us.

Lest you hear the word *confession* and picture a certain kind of religious context, know that confession on its own is part of how we're wired. Psychologically, confession actually connects us more closely to the core of our human need for love and belonging. A psychology journal notes,

> People have an unconscious compulsion to confess in
> response to real or imagined transgressions; confession thus
> provides a way to overcome feelings of guilt and remorse . . .
> [which] emanate from two sources: the fear of losing love
> and the fear of retaliation.[6]

Confession confronts our greatest vulnerabilities and helps us find stability. What if confession brings us back to security in love, just with the touch of a friend's hand or the steadiness of a shoulder?

What if sharing our deepest fears helps us trust that our most valued relationships can withstand our fears of rejection?

Confession creates space for relationship and trust in a way that appeals across impersonal screens absolutely cannot. Maybe you get to say that your confession, as hard as it was, was not nearly strong enough to break the love that was there all along. Or you just might be granted the grace to be the one who can hold out forgiveness. On the other side of confession, you may find yourself welcomed, loved, and forgiven. You may find your burdens shouldered.

You may just find yourself held.

Confession and Conviction

Confession—whether of our personal struggles or of how our hearts ache on behalf of the world—brings us into the light. It propels us out of mere frustration and into something more: truth, freedom, a life lived in the light even though the world can seem so dark.

That's part of why I share my experience with anxiety and depression. Mental health has been stigmatized in the church for too long, and I want you to know you're not alone. I encourage you to find trustworthy, caring voices: friends, licensed professional therapists, a spiritual director. Bring what you are carrying into the light. As you do, I encourage you to hold on to the promise Jesus gave his followers in John's Gospel:

> "If you abide in my word, you are truly my disciples, and
> you will know the truth, and the truth will set you free."[7]

Where we abide—or dwell—matters. If we abide in a hiding place, we cannot know the truth and be set free. But if we dwell in

Christ, the Light of the World, we will know the truth and experience a freedom that cannot compare to the safety of our hiding places.

But I also tell this part of my story as a cautionary tale of sorts.

The hard things, whether they're struggles in us or injustices we see around us, have to find their way into relationship with real lives, real hearts. If we choose to keep our thoughts to ourselves, they'll remain just ours—unformed, untested, unpurified. We need people whose wisdom and lived experience might challenge us in the best ways.

I choose to talk about anxiety and depression publicly because I've first taken that conversation into my therapist's office and to trusted friendships. Those relationships make me a better pastor, help me see my limitations (I'm not a therapist, for one!), and expand my compassion for myself and the world around me.

I choose not to debate flammable topics like abortion, immigration, or issues facing underrepresented communities without ensuring first that I'm grounded in a relationship connected to the sensitive issue. My personal rule of thumb? If I haven't taken the time to research on my own or I am not connected to an actual human being who is impacted by a topic, then I refrain from talking publicly about that issue. If that topic comes up, I confess my ignorance—that I have a long way to go—and I listen. Confession doesn't have to be followed by paragraphs of sentences. Often, silence creates space for humility and understanding.

So why risk the death to self, of pride and ego, that comes with confession? As tightrope walker Philippe Petit knew, the risk of death can actually make room for the possibility of life. This life was never meant to be lived alone. When we find ourselves on a tightrope, we should see ourselves surrounded by the beauty and complexity of community.

So *stay*.

Stay committed to real relationships. Resist the shallow and phony rhythms of disconnection, keeping words visible and lives unseen. Stay committed to the places where real is possible—and choose to speak into and from those depths. Stay committed to pushing back darkness. Confess to bring darkness into the light.

Be willing to risk your way across real tension, real tables, toward real people, real lives.

Testing the Pillar: Confession

1. What's been your personal experience with confession? Don't limit yourself to thinking of a religious context. How did you feel when you spoke the truth about yourself in community? How did you move through the conversation? What, if anything, would you do differently?

2. Why do you think it's vital to locate the issues we care about (our personal stories included) in the context of actual relationship? What potential dangers exist if we speak freely and publicly about complex and fraught topics outside the context of real relationship?

3. Read Psalm 32 and consider the three movements. Which of these movements do you imagine being easiest for you in relationship with God and others? Which one do you imagine being hardest? How are you being invited to grow in that area?

4. Has there been a time when your confession didn't go the way you intended? How did you navigate that experience?

5. What ways can you imagine the risk of confession bringing life to others?

6. Do you find silence and listening easy or difficult? What role do you think silence plays in confession?

CHAPTER 13

THE PHARMACY CLUB

[on everyday dignity]

I haven't frequented many clubs in my life. Even in my college days, the thought of getting dressed up in uncomfortable clothing and shoes just to accidentally touch sweaty people at close range for three hours made no sense to me. No, thank you. I'll take my couch, a couple of friends, and a good conversation.

Back then, though, I did know that the popular clubs were the ones with long lines out the door and around the block. They were relatively hard to get into, and yet they always seemed to have their regulars.

You know what the equivalent of that kind of club is today?

Sam's Club. The line for gas at Costco. (The hottest Sunday ticket in town!)

Even our local pharmacy is a club. You've got to show your ID (or at least give your birthday) to get in. The people that work there adhere to a strict dress code. They've got unposted hours of operation, putting up homemade signs whenever they want to take their lunch break, keeping clubgoers guessing and in suspense. At peak hours, cars are stacked one behind the other like it's a line at the local Chick-fil-A.

Up until recently, almost all our stops at The Pharmacy Club were for one of my daughters, because she's taken the same medication her entire life. When we drive by the blue and white sign, she'll scream with what sounds like misplaced excitement, "MEDCIIIIIIIIIINE!" making the word two syllables instead of three. We usually see the same three pharmacists. We know them, and they know us. We're regulars, after all.

On a recent trip to The Pharmacy Club with our oldest daughter, I pulled our car forward, rolled down my window, and saw a familiar face on the other side of the glass. Her smile was big and bright, and her dark skin glowed beneath the blue uniform vest. Her short, black hair was cropped in a modern bob, and I thought how great the new 'do looked. I realized in that same moment I was genuinely glad to see her.

"Hi, Helen!" I exclaimed through the speaker.

Helen greeted me in return and didn't even wait for me to give her our last name. After a few minutes, she came back to the window, a good pharmacy bouncer, and withheld our meds until I gave her the right birthdate. We exchanged what was needed through the sliding metal drawer, waved farewell, and off my daughter and I went.

"Mom?" she piped up from the back seat.

"Yes, honey?"

"How do you know her name?" she asked.

I paused for the briefest of moments, trying to anticipate where the conversation was headed.

"Well, she always wears a name tag. So that's how I first knew her name. But now I just know it," I replied.

There was a long silence.

"But why do you say her name like that? Why do you talk to her like you know her?"

I knew exactly why, and I hoped both my daughter and I would remember my next words for a long time.

"There are a lot of people we see, maybe not every day but regularly," I explained. "And because we don't see her every day, it'd be really easy to ignore her. But Helen is a person, and she does a very important job that means a lot to our family. So we're connected. Any time you can call someone by their first name, even if you don't know them all that well . . ."

I paused.

"It reminds both you and them that they're more than what they do, and I bet it'd mean a lot to them. Do it whenever you can."

The Pyramid of Relationships

The Flying Wallendas' seven-person pyramid is considered the most dangerous stunt in the history of circus arts. Four people balance on the wire, and stretched between each two persons' shoulders is a pole. On top of those poles stand two more people, who rest a pole between them. The last performer climbs to the top and takes a seat in a chair, rounding out the peak of the pyramid.

As they balance, even the performers who aren't directly connected in the pyramid must communicate for the stunt to go off without a hitch.[1] Constant communication, calling out how comfortable they are in their position and what they might need to hold the position longer, assures the team that each person is strong and steady, ensuring the structure will stand firm.

No matter the position or even the proximity, the strength and steadiness of one will inevitably impact all the others. Interdependence and awareness of each person determines the success of the work.

As we walk our own tightropes, seeking to steward our voices well, our work isn't just in what we choose to say, but in how we choose to uphold as valuable and worthy of respect *every single person* as we speak.

That means using our voices in relationships doesn't just apply to those in our closest circles. We must also be intentional with the other, less formalized relationships that can and do impact our lives, even if they're not relationships where we confess our deepest struggles or have the hardest conversations.

The book of 1 Peter helps guide us in this aspect of stewarding our voices. The apostle Peter is writing to persecuted church communities located in five different areas of Asia Minor.[2] He's encouraging these people in their identity as a community, because how they live together communicates to those around them what it means to be a follower of Jesus. In the verse we're going to focus on, he's outlining what it means to steward your voice as part of this identity—not just what we choose to talk about and when, but *how*:

> Treat everyone you meet with dignity. Love your spiritual family. Revere God. Respect the government.[3]

Wait a second. These churches were being persecuted, and Peter has the audacity to ask them to show proper respect . . . to *everyone*? Even those who were persecuting them? Even the government allowing the persecution?

I confess, I have a hard time imagining any of us—whether we're actually being persecuted or just feel like we are—responding that way today.

But that's the point. Choosing to treat people—to treat everyone—with dignity (in Greek, the word translated here as "treat . . . with dignity" means "to honor" or "to value") is *hard*. Because "everyone" doesn't just include kind people like Helen at the pharmacy. "Everyone" includes people we disagree with, people we find unpleasant, people who might even be doing things we find harmful.

That means choosing to be relationally countercultural even when it would be so much easier to join in with the jeers of the crowd or be silent. When your family members bash the president, you choose not to. When your girlfriends want to rag on the annoying neighbor that lives down the street, you refrain. When someone makes a racist, sexist, or homophobic comment at work, you call it out and shut it down.

Upholding and reminding others of the innate value and dignity of every human being is not always going to be easy or comfortable. That's why pursuing life in Christ isn't for the faint of heart. That's the risk of saying good.

Start with a Name

If we choose only to dignify some people and not others, the proverbial pyramid doesn't work. If it's easy for us to strip dignity away from someone else, it's just as easy for them to strip us of ours. We create an imbalance, an unequal weight, and we all fall, some of us sustaining worse injuries than others.

In her TED Talk "The Danger of a Single Story," Nigerian author Chimamanda Ngozi Adichie talks about this imbalance in terms of extracting and applying a single story—a narrative that focuses only on an isolated part of a person but then is perpetuated and applied to others as well. Adichie says,

> The consequence of the single story is this: It robs people of dignity. It makes our recognition of our equal humanity difficult. It emphasizes how we are different rather than how we are similar.[4]

So how do we emphasize our similarities instead? Adichie suggests that storytelling is a path to seeing and restoring dignity. Every person has a story. Everyday dignity looks like choosing to pay attention to and honor the story that every person carries.

And the best stories, I've come to realize, start with a name.

> Once there were four children whose names were Peter, Susan, Edmund and Lucy.
> c. s. lewis, *The Lion, The Witch and the Wardrobe*

> Mr. and Mrs. Dursley, of number four, Privet Drive, were proud to say that they were perfectly normal, thank you very much.
> j. k. rowling, *Harry Potter and the Sorcerer's Stone*

> I pulled up to the house about seven or eight and yelled to the cabbie, "Yo, homes! Smell ya later!" Looked at my kingdom, I was finally there, to sit on my throne as the prince of Bel-Air.
> will smith, *The Fresh Prince of Bel-Air* theme song

What if our one task, our one charge, is to get to know people's actual names and the stories behind them? Not what they do for work, how they voted, or which side of the tracks they're from. What if our starting point through this world—so overwhelmingly complex and divided—is to commit to say each other's names?

Names remind us of our shared humanity. Names are the foundation of everyday dignity.

This is why babies are given names, sometimes while still in the womb: to assign dignity to a life yet taking shape and still unseen.

This is why so many advocating for justice for lives lost to police brutality call out, "Say their names!"

This is why we learn the names of victims of school shootings in the United States: to reclaim the dignity of a valuable life so tragically taken away.

If we choose to learn a name in the place of "baby-killer," in the place of "thug," in the place of "pig," or "Marxist," or "freeloader"— we find ourselves at the beginning of a story. We find ourselves at the foundation of a relationship. We learn how to speak to each other because we have chosen to see each other.

To this day, we still see Helen at that pharmacy window. She knows our names, and we know hers. We smile in recognition and acknowledgment, even though a few seconds pressured by a long line is never enough to swap a good story. And I remember what I said to my daughter: "It reminds both you and them that they're more than what they do, and I bet it'd mean a lot to them. Do it whenever you can."

Choose to see people. And commit to speak their names. Do it whenever you can.

Testing the Pillar: Everyday Dignity

1. How would you characterize your interactions with people in your life that you likely see on a regular basis but don't know well? Consider baristas, restaurant workers, receptionists at your doctors' offices, and so on. Would you call those interactions intentional? Curious? Dignifying?

2. How could you bring more intentional everyday dignity to those interactions? Even if you're already regularly dignifying people, what's one extra step you could take?

3. Reread 1 Peter 2:17. Examine the apostle Peter's charge to those five churches. What's hard about heeding his charge today? What gets in the way? What do we risk if we actually choose to dignify *everyone* with our voices?

4. Take some time to journal or silently confess the ways you have torn down others' dignity or devalued them, even beyond disagreements or differences in opinion. Do this when you're unrushed and in a good place to process thoroughly.

5. Who is one person (or one group) you've labeled in an unjust way? What was the label you applied to that person or group of people? Practice using their actual name(s). What shift do you notice in yourself as you do this?

CHAPTER 14

SOMEONE'S GOING TO SEE THAT

[on legacy]

Tell your children about it in the years to come, and let your children tell their children. Pass the story down from generation to generation.

JOEL 1:3, NLT

"You're going to go back?" I ask, sounding a little more exasperated than I want to.

"Yes, I'm going back," Delwin says. "You don't have to come with me if you don't want to."

It's late. I'm sweaty. And truth be told, I'm scared for him.

"But what if it gets confrontational?" I ask.

"I won't let it," he replies.

We've just gotten home from a hangout with a group of new friends, people we played with in a recreational sports league. Another team joined us after the game for some food and good conversation. The table was a diverse one, at least racially speaking. It was nice to see so many of us—literally from two different teams—choosing to set our jerseys and loyalties aside for the sake of community.

Except part of the conversation had subtly gotten out of hand.

As one guy talked about his time overseas, he subtly suggested that people from the country he'd visited were submissive.

Then he said something about Mexicans that was out of line— and I saw my teammate look sideways, then look at me. He didn't know that she was Mexican.

Looking across the table to her, I panicked and tried to decide what to do. Would calling him out in front of a whole table of people embarrass her more? I searched her eyes to try to see how she was processing in the moment. I could tell by her body language she was annoyed and checked out.

Delwin and I left a few minutes after that, a little earlier than everyone else so we could relieve our babysitter.

On the short drive home, I tell him what happened. In our drive-way, he says, "I'm going back." His heart is set. He feels the conviction too. And though he understands why I didn't want to say anything at the table in real time, he's willing to take the chance.

I get out of the car and go inside, pacing around with a kind of nervous energy that surprises me. Why am I nervous? Am I worried about his safety? I can't deny the dynamics at play: my husband, a Black guy, up against a taller white guy. What if it ends poorly for whatever reason? Was that fear enough to hold me back? Is that why I'd stayed silent?

Sometimes silence is a way to honor what we do not know of another's experience. Sometimes silence is hurtful, a painful searing void of nothingness where someone wished we had protested, stepped in, made it right. This is where I'm still learning the delicate dance: trusting the agency and power of another to use their own voice while also choosing to discern how and when to use my own on behalf of another. Either way, it's bound to be imperfect at times.

A few minutes later, my husband returns in one piece and calmly makes his way to our bedroom.

I try to let him speak first but fail. Miserably.

"Okay, so what happened?!" I plead, a little too eagerly.

"It went fine," he responds.

This is not even close to the level of detail I'm looking for.

"Really, it went fine," he says again. "I pulled him to the side, explained to him what you'd heard and how it was racist and visibly hurt our friend's feelings. He recognized what he said was wrong . . . and he apologized profusely."

That's it?

No knock-down, drag-out, film-worthy confrontation? Although I'm glad he's safe and the conversation went well, I'm a little underwhelmed.

But also—I know that I will never forget what he did. Even more than that, I can't wait for the day when it makes sense to retell that story to our kids, pointing out not just an isolated incident but a strand of their legacy. A legacy written not on social media, but on hearts. A legacy left not for strangers but for them.

Passing It On

I'll never forget the day in my grad program when the leadership dean asked us to write our own eulogies. The classroom got quiet as he explained the sobering reality of what we'd be doing.

I didn't want to think about my own death, about how people might describe me. But the assignment gave me my first opportunity to really think about what I wanted to leave behind. What do I want my legacy to be? How am I going to move toward that?

Our voices—how and when and why we speak—are part of the

legacy we'll leave. And if we're going to leave a legacy of life and wholeness, fear cannot lead. Neither can the desire for perfection.

The night Delwin had a hard—yet successful—conversation with the man from the other team, I learned some key things about what it takes to leave a legacy with our voices:

1. **We cannot ignore the internal voices that persuade or paralyze us.** That night, I was paralyzed by fear, dissuaded from standing up for my friend because I chose to spend too much time assessing personal risk. This is something I'm learning to notice: how my internal voice impacts and restricts my external one. That voice can potentially threaten my core truths and all the things I say I value, so I need to discern when fear or perfection are speaking instead of wisdom and care.

2. **If we're using our voices in healthy, wise, relationally based ways, what we say will likely not be retweetable, shareable, or publicly visible.** No one posted about that exchange on Facebook or livestreamed about it on Instagram. My husband doesn't even know I'm telling this story right now. Using his voice wasn't about the recognition. Using his voice was about doing the right thing.

If you've mostly considered "using your voice" as code for blogging more or increasing your presence online, I hope what you're discerning now is the opposite. Yes, the ways we speak outwardly and publicly matter. But our real relationships matter more. In the end, using our voices isn't about us at all.

If and when we choose to step out on the rope of tension that lies before us, we're stepping out not for our own glory, but for a larger purpose: for unity, mutuality, restoration, and seeing things made new.

Remember: What we say matters—and so does how and *why* we say it.

Do we speak for our own glory, to attract a watching crowd? Or are we speaking to shape our here and now, making better that which we desire to pass along to the next generation, handing down our courage and convictions and faithfulness forged through the breakthroughs and mistakes we've made along the way?

So many have spoken for my good, wobbling forward to make room for me, showing me my own strength and helping me learn my own voice. I've had teachers like Mrs. Teague, who spent extra time with me after school in seventh grade to help polish speeches for competitions because she believed in my ability to say good. I've had supervisors go to bat for me in board rooms where I wasn't present, advocating for my character and competence. I've had grandmothers and aunties speak prayers, interceding on my behalf. I've had mentors forgo their own opportunities so they could give them to me, carving out space for me to listen, learn, and grow.

I learned grit from my father, an international salesman who didn't let his lack of education stop him, who understood that truly connecting with people—not just transactionally but meaningfully, sincerely—was the key to business success.

I learned how to respect people from my mother, who dignified and called by name every person she interacted with, whether they were one of her employees in corporate America or the termite guy within the four walls of our home.

I learned the power of presence from my husband, a musician, who stopped outside a frozen yogurt place on one of our first dates to intentionally listen to a young high school kid plucking away hesitantly on a guitar. He shook the kid's hand, and we spent more time than I would've liked, I admit, getting to know him.

Using our voices isn't just for us. It's for the people who are watching and learning from us. The young coworker new to our field. Those small ears and eyes watching and listening in the back seat when we least expect them to be. The friends and family members and generations after us who want to learn how we relate and stand alongside one another, how we link arms and come together to form something bigger, more stunning.

This kind of work may take a little bit of discomfort and some patience. It may take wading through the smoke of misunderstanding or situations where you feel just plain stuck.

But commit to the work, even in the small crevices of an ordinary day, and one day you just might experience how the hard work of saying good despite the complex and tense conversations pays off: the joy of a child's sweet squeal of anticipation to see a family member with whom you've worked hard to resolve tension; the gratification of processing with a loved one about a long, hard, conflict-filled day at work that you ended well; the honor of receiving an anonymous thank-you note from someone who was on the other end of your courageous stand in the face of injustice.

Each of us has been handed a legacy to carry forward with our voices. Yes, sometimes silence has its place. But writer Angie Thomas makes it plain:

What's the point of having a voice if you're gonna be silent in those moments you shouldn't be?[1]

Don't let fear keep you quiet. Do the work to prepare your voice to speak. Step forward boldly when the time comes. Then pass it on.

God's Work, Our Part

When the prophet Amos called for justice to roll down like waters, and righteousness like an ever-flowing stream,[2] that justice wasn't selective. God's work to make all things whole doesn't involve only correcting those who aren't on our side of the aisle. God's justice wasn't just for *our* brand of oppressors, those who keep our brand of truth from going forth. No—God's justice will flow to and on behalf of everyone. We cannot escape it. We will not be able to avoid our own crooked ways being made straight right alongside all the others we hoped to see corrected.

God includes all of us in the work of wholeness.

That means, one day we will all be held accountable for our participation in God's work, not just for the things we said in the face of injustice but also for what we didn't say. We'll be held accountable both for those we protected and for the vulnerable we chose to ignore. We'll see justice enacted not only *for* us but *in* us. This reality should cause us to tremble, to reconsider our ways, to pay attention to the places where God is working and we are avoiding.

Yes, no matter the part we choose to play, God is still God, and God's work moves forward. God will still be for the widow and orphan, the vulnerable children, the poor, those without food and shelter. He will still be for the marginalized and mistreated in society: women, people of color, the LGBTQ community, the incarcerated, and the unborn. He will be for Indigenous peoples and the lands upon which they lived, for immigrants, refugees, those in the disability community. He'll be for the outcasts and the downcast, for you and for me.

Justice will go forth in ways we haven't even considered. God's work of restoration will move to the ends of the earth.

Justice will be complete.

Light will shine in the darkness.

Yet it still matters how we choose to live. Salvation is an invitation to participate, a call forward to join God in God's Kingdom work. God has given us a voice and a place to use it.

And the reality is, someone needs your voice. Maybe just a couple of people around a picnic table or a kid in the back of your car—but God has a purpose and a path for you in the work of renewal, in the middle of the life you're already living.

The steps you take won't always be big. Sometimes, the next step will be quite small: one steady inch forward at a time. The work will not always be fast. Sometimes, it will be quite slow as you adjust to the gusty winds of adversarial forces. Sometimes, what you do won't be up high for all to see. Sometimes, it's low and ordinary.

Whatever you do, walk the line laid out for you. Run the good race—yours and no one else's. Step into the hope that comes alongside the courage required to say good. You may stumble, you may even fall, but don't miss out on the journey. The next generation will want to know, will need reminders of how it's done.

Certainly, there will be some who we leave behind as we walk. For many, the risk of staying will outweigh the risk of going. But hopefully when we reach our destination, we'll find that we're still face-to-face with our fellow travelers: people we love, people who were cheering us on, people we never thought we'd stick it out with, people we didn't think would stick with us.

Yes, the chasms will be there as long as we live, but that's not the grace in this story.

God's miraculous grace is that as we choose to walk across, choose to talk across tensions and heights . . .

. . . somehow, chasms turn into bridges.

Testing the Pillar: Legacy

1. Write a living eulogy: what you hope will be said about you and your voice in the world. What does this perspective affirm or reveal—not only about what or who you care about in the world but about your character and how your life uniquely lends itself to the work of all things being made new?

2. Consider how you currently steward your voice. Who is your voice for?

3. Where does your voice live? If you notice that your voice is directed more outwardly, how might you continue to steward your public voice in a healthy way? What might need to shift so you can also take part in the potentially slow, small, yet enduring work?

4. Who in your context is going to see the work you do? A child? Another family member? A friend? Imagine what your journey might mean for this person years from now. How might the ways in which you're stewarding your voice now have implications for those who come after you in one or two generations?

5. Look over your reflections from this entire book. What new themes have emerged since you started? What's one next step that you want to take before you close these pages? Invite one person to hold you accountable in that next step. If it's helpful, turn any lingering points of curiosity into questions you can bring to God over the coming weeks and months.

With Wide and Wild Thanks . . .

Every book comes to life in the midst of an author's life lived outside the pages. This book was, quite frankly, written in one of the hardest seasons of my life to date. There were days I thought I wouldn't be able to write another word or spend another minute sitting down at my laptop. There were days that my energy, my mental health—most everything—was questionable. And so it is against that cheery backdrop that I offer the most sincere thanks I know to give.

To the NavPress and Tyndale teams, particularly Caitlyn Carlson, my thorough, passionate, and wise editor and friend. Thank you for not only believing in this book but also for taking my desires to heart and making me a better writer. To Dave Zimmerman, Olivia Eldredge, Elizabeth Schroll, Deborah Gonzalez, and John Greco: Thank you all for walking with me through this season and giving me a place to land that truly feels like family. You all brought your excellence to this project. This book is in the right home, and I cannot wait to see what else we create together!

To all the NavPress authors who were part of Glen Eyrie 2023—you all are as good as they come!

To Ingrid Beck at The Bindery Agency: You are the agent that dreams are made of—kind, honest, driven, gracious. Thank you for continuing to champion me and my work.

To our Grand Rapids friends who listened and loved me so well while I was writing this book, particularly the Hatfields, Muirs, Roffs, Rhoads, Palmers, Knoesters, Kolbers, Holmes-Currans, and the entire Winning Winter crew. Thank you for nourishing my family with food when we were sick; with groceries when we were overwhelmed; with surprise joy and laughter when we were in the thick of grief. Aundi, thank you for being my book doula: for writing with me, asking questions, sending encouragement. You all are some of my favorite gifts in this life!

To Kylee, Jenny, Rhianna, and Bridgette: Thank you for being there for me across the miles, for your friendship, care, and love.

To my Colossian Forum, Pastor Camp, and Tremolo families: You all were some of my favorite parts of life while writing this book. Thank you for the sweet, sweet gifts of your presence and friendship.

To Steve Carter: I will never not take an opportunity to publicly thank you for all you've done to champion my gifts and my voice. Thank you.

To all the doctors, nurses, teachers, and caregivers who have walked with my family and me over the past couple of years: What you do matters, and the good you've both done and said mean more to me than I can capture succinctly in the back of a book.

To Kameel, Alexandria, and the amazing team at Lyon Street Café: You all created a space where I could settle in and write furiously. Thank you for your kindness—and for your amazing lattes.

To anyone who fed, welcomed, or hosted Mom and me while on Maui. Your hospitality brought my soul back to life and gave me what I needed to finish this thing!

And finally, to my family: to Mom, Delwin, Brooklyn, Myles, and Journey. You brought me countless coffees, teas, and waters while I was hiding from you in order to finish this work. You drew me pictures to encourage me. You gave me space when I needed it and cheered me through to the finish line with your smiles and hugs. If you all were words, you'd be the best words anyone could say.

Dad, I wish you could read this—but you're in these pages too. I love you!

Notes

INTRODUCTION | OUR GREAT BALANCING ACT

1. "Ahmaud Arbery: What You Need to Know about the Case," *BBC News*, November 22, 2021, https://www.bbc.com/news/world-us-canada-52623151.
2. "Ahmaud Arbery: What You Need to Know," *BBC News*.
3. Office of Public Affairs, US Department of Justice, "Federal Jury Finds Three Men Guilty of Hate Crimes in Connection with the Pursuit and Killing of Ahmaud Arbery," February 22, 2022, https://www.justice.gov/opa/pr/federal -jury-finds-three-men-guilty-hate-crimes-connection-pursuit-and-killing -ahmaud-arbery.
4. "Runners Honor Ahmaud Arbery with 2.23 Mile Run, Walk on Anniversary of His Death," *CBS News Boston*, February 23, 2021, https://www.cbsnews .com/boston/news/runners-honor-ahmaud-arbery-anniversary-death.
5. Genesis 1:1.
6. John 19:30.
7. Genesis 1:31.
8. Emily Arnold McCully, *Mirette on the High Wire* (London: Puffin Books, 1997).

CHAPTER 1 | BALANCE

1. "How to Tightrope Walk," YouTube video, 3:41, June 19, 2013, https://www .youtube.com/watch?v=9SaShn8OkJI.
2. "Because He Lives," words by Gloria Gaither and William J. Gaither, music by William J. Gaither. Copyright © 1971 Hanna Street Music (BMI) (adm. at CapitolCMGPublishing.com). All rights reserved. Used by permission.
3. Lamentations 3:22-23.
4. "The Real-World Benefits of Strengthening Your Core," Harvard Health Publishing, Harvard Medical School, January 24, 2012, https://www.health .harvard.edu/healthbeat/the-real-world-benefits-of-strengthening-your-core.

5. Katherine Rundell, "Confessions of an Amateur Tightrope Walker," *New York Times*, December 2, 2016, https://www.nytimes.com/2016/12/02/opinion/confessions-of-an-amateur-tightrope-walker.html.

6. Rundell, "Confessions of an Amateur Tightrope Walker."

7. "The Solid Rock," words by Edward Mote, music by William B. Bradbury. Public domain.

8. Damon Young, "White Tears, Explained, for White People Who Don't Get It," The Root, July 10, 2015, https://www.theroot.com/white-tears-explained-for-white-people-who-dont-get-i-1822522689.

9. Philippians 2:5-8, NRSVUE.

CHAPTER 2 | FINE-TUNING

1. Jeffrey Tayler, "A Centuries-Old Tightrope Walking Tradition Lives On in Remote Russian Villages," *National Geographic*, August 20, 2018, https://www.nationalgeographic.com/culture/article/tightrope-walking-tradition-performance-dagestan-russia-children-youth.

2. Luke 12:48, NIV.

3. Tayler, "A Centuries-Old Tightrope Walking Tradition."

4. Roopa Suchak, "World's Fastest High-Wire Walk Record Broken in China," *BBC News*, July 31, 2013, https://www.bbc.com/news/av/world-asia-china-23515577.

5. Tayler, "A Centuries-Old Tightrope Walking Tradition."

6. The film *The Social Dilemma* (2020) documents just a few of the ways our social media information is compromised.

7. James 1:19-20, NRSVUE.

8. Deuteronomy 7:21-22, NRSVUE.

9. Personal email exchange from September 25, 2020.

CHAPTER 3 | MELATONIN AND MIDNIGHT PRAYERS

1. Derald Wing Sue et al., "Racial Microaggressions in Everyday Life: Implications for Clinical Practice," *American Psychologist* 62, no. 4 (2007): 271, https://www.doi.org/10.1037/0003-066X.62.4.271.

2. Isaiah 58:9-10, 12, NIV.

3. *Merriam-Webster*, s.v. "passion (*n.*)," Word History, accessed July 17, 2023, https://www.merriam-webster.com/dictionary/passion#word-history.

4. Cahleen Shrier, "The Science of the Crucifixion," *APU Life*, March 1, 2002, https://www.apu.edu/articles/the-science-of-the-crucifixion.

5. Henri J. M. Nouwen, *The Road to Daybreak: A Spiritual Journey* (New York: Doubleday, 1988), 156.

CHAPTER 4 | MINUTES AND HOURS

1. This term is borrowed from Eugene Peterson's book *A Long Obedience in the Same Direction* (Downers Grove, IL: InterVarsity Press, 1980).
2. "Ten Thousand Hours," Spotify, track 1 on Macklemore and Ryan Lewis, *The Heist*, Macklemore, LLC, 2012.
3. Malcolm Gladwell, *Outliers: The Story of Success* (San Francisco: Little, Brown and Company, 2008), 41.
4. Tricia Hersey, *Rest Is Resistance: A Manifesto* (New York: Little, Brown Spark, 2022), 122.
5. 2 Timothy 1:6.
6. 2 Timothy 1:7, NLT.

CHAPTER 5 | EYES THAT SWEAT

1. The brief details of both the Pantaleo and Wilson cases were taken from the following article: "Wave of Protests After Grand Jury Doesn't Indict Officer in Eric Garner Chokehold Case," *New York Times*, December 3, 2014, https://www.nytimes.com/2014/12/04/nyregion/grand-jury-said -to-bring-no-charges-in-staten-island-chokehold-death-of-eric-garner .html.
2. Ashlee Eiland, "My Husband Is Eric Garner," AshleeEiland.com, December 11, 2014, https://www.ashleeeiland.com/blog/2014/12/my-husband-is-eric-garner .html.
3. Ta-Nehisi Coates, *Between the World and Me* (New York: Spiegel & Grau, 2015), 82.
4. John 11:35.
5. John 11:33.
6. *Strong's Greek Dictionary of the New Testament*, s.v. "embrimáomai" (1690), accessed via Accordance Bible Software.
7. Luke 19:42.
8. *Strong's Greek Dictionary of the New Testament*, s.v. "dakruó" (1145), accessed via Accordance Bible Software.
9. *Strong's Greek Dictionary of the New Testament*, s.v. "klaió" (2799), accessed via Accordance Bible Software.
10. Roger Lewis, "Look! No Hands and No Safety Net Either! The World's Greatest High-Wire Artiste Reveals the Secret to Walking a Tightrope at Insane Height," *Daily Mail*, December 27, 2019, https://www.dailymail .co.uk/home/books/article-7829737.
11. Psalm 92:12-14.

CHAPTER 6 | WAKE-UP CALL

1. "Wallenda Makes Grand Canyon Crossing on High Wire," *History*, This Day in History: June 23, updated June 22, 2020, https://www.history.com/this-day-in-history/wallenda-makes-grand-canyon-crossing-on-high-wire.

2. "Nik Wallenda Practice for High Wire Walk for Grand Canyon—June 7, 2013," YouTube video, 4:55 (quote at 4:13), June 7, 2013, https://www.youtube.com/watch?v=ammTtf-g6wg.

3. Rich Gallagher, "What a Tightrope Walker Can Teach Your Business," accessed August 11, 2023, https://www.carolroth.com/community/what-a-tightrope-walker-can-teach-your-business.

4. Richard J. Foster, *Celebration of Discipline: The Path to Spiritual Growth* (New York: HarperCollins, 1998), 5.

5. Foster, *Celebration of Discipline*, 1. The classical disciplines Foster names are meditation, prayer, fasting, study, simplicity, solitude, submission, service, confession, worship, guidance, and celebration.

6. Foster, *Celebration of Discipline*, 7.

7. We'll talk more about this rationale in the section on the Relationship Pillar.

8. H. L. Ellison, "The Gospel According to Matthew," in *Zondervan Bible Commentary*, ed. F. F. Bruce (Grand Rapids, Michigan: Zondervan, 2008), 1070.

9. Ellison, "Matthew," *Zondervan Bible Commentary*, 1071.

10. Matthew 7:4-5, MSG.

CHAPTER 7 | FROZEN IN TIME

1. This brief history of Maria Spelterini's walk was adapted from the following article: Don Redmond, "Only One Woman Has Walked the Tightrope over Niagara Falls—But She Did It Five Times in 19 Days," In Niagara Region (insauga.com), March 8, 2023, https://www.insauga.com/only-one-woman-has-walked-the-tightrope-over-niagara-falls-but-she-did-it-5-times-in-19-days.

2. William Shakespeare, *Julius Caesar*, act 4, sc. 3, http://shakespeare.mit.edu/julius_caesar/julius_caesar.4.3.html.

3. B. L. Wilson, "I'm Your Black Friend, but I Won't Educate You about Racism. That's on You," *The Washington Post*, June 8, 2020, https://www.washingtonpost.com/outlook/2020/06/08/black-friends-educate-racism.

4. See Mark 2:1-12.

5. Mark 2:5, NIV.

6. Mark 2:12, NIV.

CHAPTER 8 | FIX YOUR FACE

1. Lee Rainie et al., "Trust and Distrust in America," Pew Research Center, July 22, 2019, https://www.pewresearch.org/politics/2019/07/22/americans-struggles-with-truth-accuracy-and-accountability.

2. Rainie et al., "Trust and Distrust in America."

3. Mark 10:17, NIV.

4. "What Does Mark 10:18 Mean?" Got Questions Ministries, BibleRef, accessed July 20, 2023, https://www.bibleref.com/Mark/10/Mark-10-18.html.

5. Mark 10:21.

6. *Encyclopaedia Britannica Online*, s.v. "Agape," updated July 5, 2023, https://www.britannica.com/topic/agape.

7. Mark 10:21.

CHAPTER 9 | "SEARCH MAPS"

1. "Rwandan Genocide," *History*, updated May 19, 2023, https://www.history.com/.amp/topics/africa/rwandan-genocide.

2. This phrase is enshrined on a plaque at the Kigali Genocide Memorial; visited July 24, 2019.

3. "The Rwanda Genocide," United States Holocaust Memorial Museum, Washington, DC, updated April 5, 2021, https://encyclopedia.ushmm.org/content/en/article/the-rwanda-genocide.

4. Megan Specia, "How a Nation Reconciles after Genocide Killed Nearly a Million People," *New York Times*, April 25, 2017, https://www.nytimes.com/2017/04/25/world/africa/rwandans-carry-on-side-by-side-two-decades-after-genocide.html.

5. Laura Clark, "The Russian Village Entirely Populated by Tightrope Walkers," *Smithsonian Magazine*, Smart News, February 24, 2015, https://www.smithsonianmag.com/smart-news/russian-village-entirely-populated-tightrope-walkers-180954391.

6. Nathan Oates, *Stability: How an Ancient Monastic Practice Can Restore Our Relationships, Churches, and Communities* (Brewster, MA: Paraclete Press, 2021), 83–84.

7. Jonathan Jones, "The Most Transient American Cities," Construction Coverage, updated May 24, 2023, https://constructioncoverage.com/research/most-transient-us-cities.

8. Jeremiah 29:7, NIV.

9. Defined as "a theology lived in the context of an unconditional commitment to a particular neighborhood or community." See Wayne Gordon and John M. Perkins, *Making Neighborhoods Whole: A Handbook for Christian Community Development* (Downers Grove, IL: InterVarsity Press, 2013), 51.

10. Gordon and Perkins, *Making Neighborhoods Whole*, 49.

CHAPTER 10 | VERIFIED

1. "What Is the Writer's Voice? How to Find Your Writing Voice," MasterClass, updated September 29, 2021, https://www.masterclass.com/articles/how-to-find-your-writing-voice.

2. 1 Corinthians 12:15-17, NASB.
3. "BGT Dog Gets Death Threats after Stunt Double," *BBC News*, June 7, 2015, https://www.bbc.com/news/newsbeat-33040782.
4. Leslie Jamison, "Why Everyone Feels Like They're Faking It," *New Yorker*, February 6, 2023, https://www.newyorker.com/magazine/2023/02/13/the -dubious-rise-of-impostor-syndrome.
5. Jamison, "Why Everyone Feels Like They're Faking It."
6. Ruchika Tulshyan and Jodi-Ann Burey, "Stop Telling Women They Have Imposter Syndrome," *Harvard Business Review*, February 11, 2021, https://hbr .org/2021/02/stop-telling-women-they-have-imposter-syndrome.

CHAPTER 11 | PANDEMIC PUPPY AND PAUL (AGAIN)

1. Rick Laezman, "Electricians, Tightrope Walker Team Up for High-Wire Act," *Electrical Contractor*, August 15, 2013, https://www.ecmag.com/magazine /articles/article-detail/your-business-electricians-tightrope-walker-team -high-wire-act.
2. Caitlin Killoren, "3 Types of Power Dynamics in a Relationship (And How to Find a Balance)," *Relish*, December 23, 2021, https://hellorelish.com/articles /relationship-power-dynamics.html.
3. Nihar Chhaya, "How to Figure Out the Power Dynamics in a New Job," *Harvard Business Review*, August 29, 2022, https://hbr.org/2022/08/how -to-figure-out-the-power-dynamics-in-a-new-job.
4. Sonia Torres Rodríguez et al., "Changing Power Dynamics among Researchers, Local Governments, and Community Members: A Community Engagement and Racial Equity Guidebook," PDF, Urban Institute, June 2022, https://www .urban.org/sites/default/files/2022-06/cem-guidebook-print.pdf.
5. 1 Corinthians 12:19-20, 22-24, MSG. Italics in the original.
6. Jaimee Bell, "The Signs of Unhealthy Power Dynamics in a Relationship— and How to Even Them Out," Big Think, February 20, 2022, https://bigthink .com/neuropsych/power-in-relationships.

CHAPTER 12 | NOT-SO-HAPPY HOUR

1. "Seasonal Affective Disorder," National Institute of Mental Health, accessed August 18, 2023, https://www.nimh.nih.gov/health/publications/seasonal -affective-disorder.
2. Psalm 32:3.
3. Psalm 32:5.
4. See Ephesians 4:32.
5. Galatians 6:2.

6. Saul M. Kassin and Gisli H. Gudjonsson, "The Psychology of Confessions: A Review of the Literature and Issues," *Psychological Science in the Public Interest* 5, no. 2 (November 2004), 33–67, https://doi.org/10.1111/j.1529-1006.2004.00016.x.

7. John 8:31-32.

CHAPTER 13 | THE PHARMACY CLUB

1. "Nik Wallenda Performs 7-Person Pyramid, Months after Relatives Were Injured During Stunt, *Inside Edition*, updated October 28, 2017, https://www.insideedition.com/nik-wallenda-performs-7-person-pyramid-months-after-relatives-were-injured-during-stunt-37600.

2. *Encyclopaedia Britannica*, s.v. "Letters of Peter," updated August 21, 2020, https://www.britannica.com/topic/letters-of-Peter.

3. 1 Peter 2:17, MSG.

4. Chimamanda Ngozi Adichie. "The Danger of a Single Story," TED Video, 18:33 (quote begins at 13:46), TEDGlobal 2009, https://www.ted.com/talks/chimamanda_ngozi_adichie_the_danger_of_a_single_story.

CHAPTER 14 | SOMEONE'S GOING TO SEE THAT

1. Angie Thomas, *The Hate U Give* (London: Walker Books, 2018), 166.

2. See Amos 5:24.

NavPress is the book-publishing arm of The Navigators.

Since 1933, The Navigators has helped people around the world bring hope and purpose to others in college campuses, local churches, workplaces, neighborhoods, and hard-to-reach places all over the world, face-to-face and person-by-person in an approach we call Life-to-Life® discipleship. We have committed together to know Christ, make Him known, and help others do the same.®

Would you like to join this adventure of discipleship and disciplemaking?

- Take a Digital Discipleship Journey at **navigators.org/disciplemaking**.
- Get more discipleship and disciplemaking content at **thedisciplemaker.org**.
- Find your next book, Bible, or discipleship resource at **navpress.com**.

 @NavPressPublishing

 @NavPress

 @navpressbooks